Rare Beasts, Unique Adventures

At last! A first-rate devotional book for college students that deals squarely with the problems they face daily, and in the rich context of the classics of Christian devotional literature. The author is an expert on faith development and well-published in America's leading magazines.

—Dean Ebner, Dean of the College Faculty, North Park College

A warm and wonderful book; a sparkling, captivating introduction to some of the most fascinating people the community of faith has to offer, and a delightful guide for daily life.

—Mitch Finley, author of *Catholic Spiritual Classics* and *Married Love: A Special Way of Being Alive*

This is more than a devotional for college students; more than sage advice. It is a book that brings together the real lives of students with the personal stories and writings of many who have walked this way before and with the Loving God who shares the journey. No pat answers here, but an invitation to make an exciting pilgrimage of faith through the college years.

—Stephen A. Hayner, President, InterVarsity Christian Fellowship

Linda Lawrence has done a super job of writing meditations that will serve as a primer for all college students who desire to let Christ make a difference in their lives and the lives of others. As a side benefit, readers will be exposed to a wide variety of authors and ideas that will stimulate them to read more C. S. Lewis, Thomas Merton, Frederick Buechner, Dietrich Bonhoeffer, and Martin Luther King, Jr.

—Scott Dimock, Young Life, Eastern Division

Still looking for those elusive thousand points of light? From her deeply felt experiences as an educator Linda Lawrence has found them, often in the persons of courageous and resourceful students who overcame what can be the cruel crucible of college life to give hope to their peers—an inspiration to all of us.

—James McDermott, Senior Editor, *Guideposts*

What a find! Linda Lawrence's devotional reader for college students is a chaplain's delight. It is intelligent, timely, alert to

student needs, and faithful to the biblical witness. This is something practical but profound that I will recommend to students as a daily guide for spiritual nurture and responsible living. Her use of the Bible, student voices, and Christian writings throughout the ages is highly stimulating.

—William D. Apel, Chaplain and Professor of Religion, Linfield College

This wide-ranging collection of stories and reflections will provide both stimulation of the mind and confirmation of the deepest impulses of the human heart and thereby be good company for contemporary college students—from both Protestant and Roman Catholic traditions—as they move through the adventure and promise of a college education and must compose a viable and vital adult faith.

—Sharon Parks, Harvard University

I learned from this book what I had already observed on campus: Linda Lawrence loves college students. The range of her knowledge of their lives, her sensitivity to their main purposes, and her warm Christian faith iradiate these pages. This book would make a splendid college companion.

—F. Dale Bruner, Wasson Professor of Religion, Whitworth College

I wish I had read this book during my own college experience to help give words to describe the pain of broken attachments and bitter assumptions, and to inspire me to receive the promise that college life embraced.

—Kathy Harrell Storm, Professor of Psychology, Calvin College

Linda Lawrence has crafted a wonderful, valuable resource for the college student's oft-times bumpy journey. She writes as she acts, fascinated with people, curious, probing, always ready to engage in honest, down-to-earth conversation.

—Richard I Ferrin, President, Maryville College

RARE
BEASTS
UNIQUE
ADVENTURES

Reflections for College Students

Linda Lawrence

 ZondervanPublishingHouse
Grand Rapids, Michigan

A Division of HarperCollins*Publishers*

Rare Beasts, Unique Adventures: Reflections for College Students
Copyright © 1991 by Linda Lawrence Hunt

Requests for information should be addressed to:
Zondervan Publishing House
1415 Lake Drive, S.E.
Grand Rapids, Michigan 49506

Library of Congress Cataloging-in-Publication Data

Lawrence, Linda, 1940–
    Rare beasts, unique adventures / Linda Lawrence.
      p.   cm.
   ISBN 0-310-53271-X
   Includes bibliographical references.
   1. College students—Prayer-books and devotions—English.
I. Title.
BV4531.2L397 1991
242'.634–dc20   90-23951
                                                 CIP

We wish to thank the following publishers for use of their material: "For the Time Being: A Christmas Oratorio," from the *Collected Poems of W. H. Auden* by W. H. Auden. Copyright © 1976 by Edward Mendelson, William Meredith, and Monroe K. Spears, executors of the estate of W. H. Auden. Reprinted by permission of Random House, Inc. The poem by Wendell Berry on page 95 is from *Sayings and Doings and an Eastward Look* and is reprinted by permission of Gnomon Press.

All Scripture quotations, unless otherwise noted, are taken from the *Holy Bible: New International Version* (North American Edition). Copyright © 1973, 1978, 1984, by the International Bible Society. Used by permission of Zondervan Bible Publishers.

Interior design: Rachel Hostetter
Cover design: Gary Gnidovic
Cover illustration: Tamata Norrgard

Printed in the United States of America

91 92 93 94 95 96 / AK / 10 9 8 7 6 5 4 3 2 1

*To students
at Whitworth College
and beyond
who told their truths
with such openness*

CONTENTS

He is the Way,
Follow Him through the Land of Unlikeness
And you will see rare beasts,
And have unique
Adventures

W. H. Auden, Christmas Oratorio

ACKNOWLEDGMENTS

There is an African proverb: "Because we are, I am—I am, because we are." The simple fact is, we need community. Writing a book, especially one that depends so heavily on other people's stories, helps me realize that need. Perhaps because writing is often a lonely act, I've sensed the companionship. In condensing their lives, I hope I've stayed true to their spirits.

I want to give special thanks to:

- The students at Whitworth College, and on other campuses across America, who trusted me with parts of their stories. Their names have been changed to provide privacy.
- Colleagues and friends who generously added their insights on the college world, loaned books from their personal libraries, and gave me needed encouragement in the writing: Forrest Baird, Lee Anne Chaney, Barbara Filo, Marianne and Ron Frase, Kathleen Hume, Lois Kieffaber, Doris and Don Liebert, Martha Nelson, Marty Erb, Leonard Oakland; and the supportive English department faculty, Sharon Daloz Parks, Lura Pierce, Tammy Reid, Jerry Sittser, and Brett Webb Mitchell.
- The "rare beasts" included here, whose beliefs overcame their doubts so that their personal encounter with the Holy could be written down for others. Although many others were left out, they still kept me company while thinking and writing.
- My Mom and Dad, Evelyn and Harold Christensen. They nurtured my brother, Larry, and me with such love that the biblical idea of an extended family of God sounded most inviting.
- The exceptional library staff at Whitworth, who combed the nation for books and patiently nudged me during late returns. Also, the fine library at First Presbyterian Church in Spokane offered excellent resources.

• Our college-aged son and daughters, Jeff, Susie, and Krista, who along with their friends, give me high hopes for the vitality and faith spirits of their generation.

• Thoughtful editor Bob Hudson, who expressed confidence from the beginning of the project and candid critiques through to its conclusion.

• My husband, Jim, a history professor who shares my love of biography. His constant, steady support gave our family much needed attention during demanding months.

Two drawbacks in this slim book bear mentioning. First, since college experiences are as varied as life itself, many significant topics have been left out. I welcome hearing more from you; perhaps these topics can be included in future editions. Second, many of the writers quoted in this book lacked a sensitivity to gender issues. Although I wish their language reflected their inclusive spirits, out of respect for their voices, their quotations have not been altered.

INTRODUCTION

▌ still remember the September afternoon a student gave me the idea for this book. Knowing that 40 percent of all college students drop out, I had been interviewing seniors across America trying to find out what the other 60 percent shared in common. Why did they succeed in reaching their goals despite meeting the same difficulties as those who quit? What inner resources did they draw on during times of discouragement?

In one interview, Scott, a lanky, creative senior in my advanced writing class at Whitworth College, described his freshman year. In many ways, he had entered college destined for failure. But not only did he graduate, he was accepted into one of the nation's most prestigious seminaries.

"I had lousy study habits," Scott explained, "no financial or emotional support from my divorced parents, nor any idea what I wanted to study. I wasn't even sure why I came." But two things helped him during his shaky first year: "Every day I grabbed my devotional book and found fifteen minutes to think—even if it was in the bathroom. Some of my best ideas came during these quiet times."

A few Christian friends also provided support and stretched his vision. Most were other students simply trying to live out their faith in the ways they studied, dated, spent money, worshiped, and related to others in their school and community. These students caused Scott to rethink his choices. Then, when he traveled to Latin America for a semester service-study program, he experienced what it meant to be welcomed into the international family of faith: "It didn't matter if they were Protestant or Catholic, church leaders or peasants I met in local Bible studies, or other college Christians—we knew we loved the same God. They gave me new lenses to see the world."

These new dimensions completely altered Scott's life—the kind of adventure that writer Eugene Peterson so well described:

The word *Christian* means different things to different people. To one person it means a stiff, upright, inflexible way of life, colorless and unbending. To another it means a risky, surprise-filled venture, lived tiptoe at the edge of expectation (Romans 8). If we get our information from the biblical material, there is no doubt that the Christian life is a dancing, leaping, daring life.

My hope is that this book, *Rare Beasts, Unique Adventures,* will be a challenging companion to you during college, providing mentors and friends for the journey. The title comes from W. H. Auden's *Christmas Oratorio*:

> He is the Way,
> Follow Him through the Land of Unlikeness
> And you will see rare beasts,
> And have unique
> Adventures

Some people suggest that college is an unlikely land for faith to grow, that it's easy for students to lose their faith. But as I listen to students at both large state universities and smaller church-related or independent liberal-arts colleges, it is precisely the turmoil and challenge of these years that many say most shapes their spiritual growth.

For students wanting such a challenge, these years can be a surprise-filled faith adventure. No longer able to turn to family or long-time friends for support, no longer content with easy answers to complex problems, and no longer as willing to let popular culture mold their character, many students enter into a closer encounter with God. Simply stated, they find they need to pray. But these students seldom grow in isolation; they need connections with other Christians. You'll meet some of these students and hear how they attempt to live a creative faith during their college years.

It isn't easy. Other values compete for your allegiance—some subtle, some not so subtle. Recently television director Norman Lear addressed the Harvard Business School graduates and spoke of America's spiritual crisis and climate of self-centeredness:

> America's obsession with short-term thinking and corrosive individualism is at the expense of the human spirit. We

need leaders who can think of the future ... the common good of the community ... who want to leave something lasting behind.

When I was a student with a fairly young faith at the University of Washington, I started reading biographies of believers and discovered that we have been called to join a wonderful extended family of faith. Inevitably, the lives of these believers offered fresh-spirited ways of understanding the challenge to become the people of God in a wounded world. Throughout this book you will meet many "rare beasts" of the historic and contemporary Christian community whose example and words have left something lasting. If you want to read more, a list of books is included after the conclusion.

Don't worry—these people are far from perfect. They are ordinary men and women who embraced the call of Christ to "love the Lord your God with all your heart and with all your soul and with all your mind and with all your strength [and] your neighbor as yourself."

In distinctive ways, their faith commitments led them into unique adventures across the world. In staying open to God's mysterious leading, Martin Luther King, Jr., traveled the treacherous streets of Selma, Alabama, and flew to Oslo, Norway, to accept the Nobel Peace Prize. Annie Dillard lived in a San Juan Island beach cabin and linked the minute wonders of the natural world with her search to understand the Holy. While raising her family, award-winning author Madeleine L'Engle moved away from the cultural vitality of New York City and discovered quieter truths in the rhythms of a rural Connecticut village. Dietrich Bonhoeffer, a young German pastor and author of *The Cost of Discipleship*, found his road leading to a Berlin jail cell when the Nazis suspected his involvement in the resistance movement against Hitler. C. S. Lewis, who stayed in the same home in England for many years, found his imagination roaming into the Land of Narnia, and he created books for children that are now cherished around the world. Mother Teresa left her comfortable teaching position and began a hospice ministry in the slums of Calcutta. Working with the poorest of the poor, each day she determines to do "something beautiful for God."

Our creator has given us an extraordinary call—to love him with all the fullness of our lives. While studying my Spanish Bible, I noticed that the word *bienaventurada,* usually translated "blessed," could easily be read as "good adventurer." In a sense, that's appropriate, for if we are good adventurers in faith, our lives will be blessed.

My hope is that you will find the college years a rich "land of unlikeness" and discover how good an adventure really can be. Enjoy!

MATTERS
OF
THE
HEART

Introduction: Love at the Center ◙

Thou hast made us for Thyself and our hearts are restless until they rest in Thee.   ST. AUGUSTINE

From the moment you step onto campus, your heart will be pulled toward many allegiances, each clamoring for your loyalty, each parading promises of the good life. Some are obvious. "Come," they will beckon, "and give your heart to career goals, academics, romance, athletic achievement, performing arts, peer groups, friendships." What is so confusing is that each of these has positive values and is worthy of effort. But are they worthy of our trust? Are they worth centering our lives on?

Many students tell me no—but often only after one of these unpredictable centers shatters. Sometimes it breaks in a split second; sometimes it fractures with a slow fissure. I think of Mark, a star catcher, hobbling into class on crutches. One bad move snapped cartilage and ligaments, detouring his long-held dream of professional baseball. Or Sally, who two months before her wedding, found her four-year investment in a romance broken with the words, "I just don't think I'm ready." For Susan it came at the end of her sophomore year when her four best friends all transferred to different schools. "Suddenly," she said, "I felt like a friendless freshman again, needing to start over."

Each of these students had to reconsider their priorities once they saw the fragility of what they trusted in as the center of their lives. The call to "love God with all our heart" is not just a belief in an abstract theological idea, nor a demand, but a dazzling invitation to enter into a relationship with the Living God. And the warmest, strongest quality of friendship is required: the giving of our heart to Another. This is seldom easy.

The cowardly lion in the *The Wizard of Oz* understood this. A person needs courage—exactly what the lion sorely lacked. Tired of his timid spirit, he embarked on a long search for a brave, courageous, adventurous spirit. He wouldn't settle for living with less—or fulfilling Thoreau's observation that "most men live lives of quiet desperation."

In a complex, always challenging, college environment, God offers the chance to live with Love at the center, giving strength and peace during a restless journey. Christ says, "Come to me, all you who are weary and burdened, and I will give you rest" (Matthew 11:28). For those who choose to come, there is a promise of inner strength—"that you may be strengthened in your inner being with power through his Spirit, and that Christ may dwell in your hearts through faith, as you are being rooted and grounded in love" (Ephesians 3:16–17 *New Revised Standard Version*). The word *come* implies choice. Our God does not force allegiance, for then it would not be love.

The Danish philosopher Søren Kierkegaard also understood this. He wrestled with the fact that Christianity isn't simply a theory but "must be taken up into my life to be meaningful." He wrote:

> What good would it do me to be able to explain the
> meaning of Christianity if it had no deeper significance for
> me and my life; what good would it do me if truth stood
> before me, cold and naked, not caring whether I recognized
> her or not, and producing in me a shudder of fear rather
> than a trusting devotion? . . . But it must be taken up into
> my life, and that is what I now recognize as the most
> important thing. That is what my soul longs after, as the
> African desert thirsts for water.

As Kierkegaard knew, when Jesus says, "If anyone hears my voice and opens the door, I will come in and eat with him, and he with me" (Revelation 3:20), Jesus leaves us fully free to decide whether we will open the door to such a relationship. First and foremost it is an act of the *will* and an answer to the questions: "What do we want?" and "On what or who do we want to center

MATTERS OF THE HEART

our lives?" It is not to be confused with emotions, which inevitably roller-coaster up and down.

To love the Lord with all our heart also leads us to loosen our attachments to the world's values. It isn't just positive values like friendship, athletics, and romance that can draw our loyalties. There is another side of our hearts—the dark side—that the Bible speaks about with frank realism. As Jesus said, "Out of the heart come evil thoughts, murder, adultery, sexual immorality, theft, false testimony, slander" (Matthew 15:19–20). Or as the writer of Proverbs advises: "Guard your heart, for it is the wellspring of life" (4:23).

One of the struggles students face is seeing beyond the powerful allure of outwardly attractive options that may prove destructive to the heart. Almost always the attraction stems from the assurance of immediate, short-lived pleasure: the momentary high promised by mind-altering drugs, the buzz from booze, or the sensual stimulation of no-commitment sex. Some of the "rare beasts" in this book—like Augustine and Kierkegaard—tried some of these things too, but the allure of temporal pleasure simply couldn't hold them.

Augustine and Kierkegaard each came to a point where they asked for a new heart; they came to a place where they could rest in a changeless Center of love. In their own way they repeated the prayer of the psalmist: "Create in me a pure heart, O God, and renew a steadfast spirit within me" (Psalm 51:10). And both received the ancient, trustworthy promise given to Ezekiel: "I will give you a new heart and put a new spirit in you; I will remove from you your heart of stone and give you a heart of flesh. And I will put my spirit in you" (36:26–27).

What characterizes this new heart? The angel's first words to Mary and the shepherds, announcing God's gift of love, were "Be not afraid." In other words, courage is essential. And what changes a timid heart into a courageous heart? The call to compassion— letting love cast out fear. "We love because he first loved us" (1 John 4:19). It's the courage the lion in *The Wizard of Oz* longed for and searched for—and he would have been ecstatic!

Thomas Kelly, the twentieth-century Quaker and author of *Testament of Devotion,* speaks of this new spirit of compassion. "He plucks the world out of our hearts, loosening the chains of attachment. And He hurls the world into our hearts, where we and He together carry it in infinite tender love." It is this "hurling the world into our hearts" that gives us hearts of courage to see the world through the new light of God's love. It is not an "attachment to" but a "love for" that is far greater than our own finite view.

College students committed to following God's direction show courage in very specific daily acts of faith. Once they have set their will, they try not to let unruly emotions control them. I think of Bev, who was fascinated by science and believed a career in science would offer her unlimited ways to serve the world. But when she took her first math class, essential for her major, she discovered her high-school training had been woefully inadequate. Also, her professor, though brilliant, lacked the skills to help a floundering freshman. Bev failed math her first semester. She felt discouraged and stupid.

Typically when students fail a course in their major, they think they have chosen that major poorly, so they shift their interests. Not Bev. She promptly signed up to repeat the math class the second semester, this time checking the student grapevine to find out which teachers might be more helpful to weaker students, and Bev also found a tutor. Four years later she graduated in biology and immediately found a research position.

Other students resist letting fear determine their decisions. One woman was convinced that God had called her to the ministry, but she hated public speaking. It terrified her. So she took one speech course after another in an attempt to calm her fears and learn this essential skill. If she had placed a 4.0 grade average at the center of her life, she would never have pursued her dream.

It takes social courage as well. I think of Shawn, a committed Christian who lived in a fraternity where he built strong friendships even though he chose not to follow the drinking norms. And I think of Randi, a thirty-eight-year-old woman returning to college, who felt so intimidated at a university of 38,000 students that every day for a week she drove to campus, sat in the car, and simply watched the students from the parking lot.

Finally, she gained the confidence to register for classes the following term. Eventually, she earned a master's degree.

I also see the courage of compassion in many students' lives: volunteering in their communities in places of need; gently helping a drunk roommate sober up; listening to a troubled friend; explaining a hard economics problem to another student; writing letters to free political prisoners through Amnesty International.

Part of a relationship with the Living God is gaining a new heart that grows in courage and compassion. We are told, "Today, if you hear his voice, do not harden your hearts" (Psalm 95:7–8). This is the grand invitation—to open our hearts to Love. ◙

Leaving Home ◧

The Lord had said to Abram, "Leave your country, your people and your father's household and go to the land I will show you."   GENESIS 12:1

When Maria, a young Hispanic woman from Colorado, traveled 1,500 miles from home to attend college in the Northwest, she didn't come alone. Her warm extended family— grandma, grandpa, mom, dad, and brothers—drove with her.

Maria knew no one in this new land, and after the family helped her unpack, they started the difficult good-byes. "You've made us very proud," said her grandpa. "You're the first in our family to go to college."

"I love you," said her dad, unable to say more as he hugged his only daughter good-bye.

"If you ever need anything," said her tiny grandma, "just give us a call, and we'll do what we can."

But it was her mom's words that Maria most remembered during her first difficult month: "We will miss you, Maria, but we would never take away from you what we cannot give you—and that is your education. God has given you the power to be whatever you want to be. You've been given the gift of being smart and God intends for you to use it."

Then, before climbing into the car, her mom added, "Get the most out of college and don't back down from any challenges God puts in your path. I know you'll make it with God's help."

During the next several days of almost overwhelming loneliness, heightened by an uncomfortable roommate situation, her mom's words echoed in her mind. Maria recalled, "I had to keep remembering: 'Don't back down from any challenges God puts in your path.' I was terribly disorganized. I lost my meal card, my purse, my class schedule, and other things. I just hated being away from my friends, family, and Colorado. Lots of nights I just wanted to climb on a plane and go home."

But slowly she began to enjoy her new independence. "I had to transfer my trust to God in ways I'd never had to before in my protected, secure environment. My faith took on completely new dimensions."

Chad, who took a class with Maria, couldn't understand her loneliness at all. He could hardly wait to get out of his house his senior year. He drove a thousand miles to college by himself, instantly felt at home and made good friends. "I was surprised at how much I didn't miss home. I just loved being on my own and did well in classes." When he went home to California for Christmas, he thought he had made all his adjustments.

But to Chad's complete surprise, when he returned for winter term, his first gnawing sense of homesickness hit. "I think leaving the sunshine and beach, and returning to cold and snow was what first got to me. I started thinking about home and family and friends all the time." Finally, he got so depressed he told his dad how he felt. "I actually was tempted to quit and go home."

"Hey, that's okay, Chad," responded his dad. "When I was a freshman, I suddenly decided to drive fifteen hundred miles home for Thanksgiving. It's a normal feeling."

In learning to live in a strange land, both Maria and Chad joined in an adventure similar to the one God asked of many faithful followers in biblical times—sojourners like Abraham and Sarah, Ruth, Joseph and Mary, the disciples, and Paul. It's a "going without knowing"—into a future filled with mystery. It makes one wonder, *Are there things that can only be learned from being "on the road"*? An adventure implies risk—but God's great promise is that we are never alone. As Hebrews 13:5–6 states, "God has said, 'Never will I leave you; never will I forsake you.' So we say with confidence, 'The Lord is my helper; I will not be afraid.'"

Where do you most need to trust God in your new land? Is there a specific fear or challenge along your path you can turn over to God in prayer? Do you enjoy adventure and change? Or, if you enjoy adventure and change, can you be a sensitive friend to those finding transitions difficult? ▣

Rejection ◙

*When I found out my high-school girlfriend was sleeping
with my best friend, I skipped classes and drank solid for
two weeks.*   A FIRST-YEAR STUDENT

I couldn't believe it; I didn't make the choir list.
                                A TALENTED MUSIC STUDENT

On every college campus, every day and night,
students get stung with rejection. For Sally, it happened when her
"best friend" from first semester chose to snub her second
semester. For Jennifer, it happened the day before classes began at
a large university, when the sororities of her choice dropped her
during the final selection process. For Stan, a twenty-six-year-old
senior, it occurred when the education department refused him
admission into student teaching for "personality inadequacies" that
the department felt would hurt his effectiveness in the classroom.
Add to such rejections the normal making and breaking of
campus romances and the ups and downs of grades—and it's
obvious why the heart of any college student needs to be resilient.

For Christ, it occurred when Peter, a disciple he loved and
trusted, denied three times that he had even known him! "I do not
know the man," he insisted while Jesus was being tortured before
his crucifixion. How much more this rejection must have hurt
than even the public humiliation of being treated like a common
criminal. But fortunately for Peter, that wasn't the end of the
story.

"Rejection is what you make it," said one senior. "It happens
all the time, but it can lead to better understanding of yourself and
others. And often it leads to something better. There's some truth
in the idea that for every door that closes, a window opens."

After her initial hurt from her former best friend, Sally
decided to take a good look at her own friendship patterns. "I had

put all my trust in her; I told her secrets I'd never shared with anyone and planned all my time around her schedule. I'd shut out other people if they conflicted with our plans. The truth was, I was dependent, and she was understandably tired of it." From then on, Sally started to build a larger network of friends and now finds her college experience to be far richer.

Jennifer eventually dropped out of the university she had originally selected largely for its big-name prestige value. She took an honest look at her need for community and re-enrolled at a smaller college where dorm life provided this.

For Stan, the education department's evaluation threw him into turmoil for weeks and forced him into a fundamental reevaluation of his career goals. Reluctantly, he took advantage of the university's career-counseling center and took tests to determine his natural talents, aptitudes, and interests. The results reaffirmed his interest in working with children, but also indicated that he probably would function much better one-on-one than in a classroom situation. He shifted to child psychology with a new goal of becoming a school counselor.

And Christ, looking beyond the hurt of his rejection, showed Peter the depth of God's unconditional love and forgiveness. He gave Peter the chance to restate his love three times (see John 21:15–17). Then he commissioned him to tell the story of God's unending love and faithfulness—something Peter could then understand in fresh ways.

Rejection shouldn't surprise us. Love and pain are always intermingled. But when it happens, we have the choice to take our hurts, large and small, and place them before the One who wants to heal them. Or we can live lives of self-pity, clinging to our rejection as an excuse for never risking anything again.

Almost always, healing takes time—sometimes a long time. Yet time also brings some wonderful twists and turns to our lives, directed by a wiser hand than our own. God's promise is that "he heals the brokenhearted and binds up their wounds" (Psalm 147:3). When you encounter the slammed door of rejection, can you find the slim window that opens to healing the hurt? ◨

Truth or
Consequences ◙

*Those who say that religion has nothing to do with politics
do not know what religion means.*   MAHATMA GANDHI

*To see the earth as it truly is, small and blue and
beautiful, in that eternal silence where it floats, is to see
ourselves as riders on the earth together, brothers on that
loveliness in the eternal cold, brothers that know now they
are truly brothers.*   POET ARCHIBALD MACLEISH

At times your convictions may collide with society's
norms. It isn't always your conviction that determines whether
something is acceptable or not, but the community's prevailing
values.

For example, a student may feel compelled to speak publicly
in support of anti-abortion legislation. On some campuses that
view would be the popular and "politically correct" one and would
take little courage to voice. At another university, however, it
could be considered old-fashioned and unthinking, an attempt by
that student to impose his or her beliefs on others. Bucking such a
tide takes considerable courage.

Now reverse the situation. Consider the student who voices a
pro-choice position because of his or her honest convictions. Again,
on some university campuses, this would take no courage—and
that student would be within the norms of "community think."
But on another campus, where the values reflect a prevailing belief
linking the Christian faith with a fervent anti-abortion position,
expressing a pro-choice view could bring collective scorn.

Consider U.S. Senator Mark Hatfield from Oregon, who
knows what it feels like to go against a popular position. In his
book *Between a Rock and a Hard Place,* he recounts his

transformation from popular governor of Oregon in the sixties, where the press predicted this handsome young politician would be "presidential timber," to a highly controversial U.S. senator who led the early opposition to the Vietnam War. As a Baptist known for his commitment to the Christian faith, he received tremendous criticism from conservative church members who considered his opposition to the war highly un-American.

But his opposition was neither political nor strategic. "It came intuitively, emotionally, from my depths," explains Hatfield, who found his reaction was shaped profoundly by his experiences as a military officer in World War II. He was among the first outsiders to view the atomic destruction in Hiroshima in September 1945. "The devastation I saw in Hiroshima seemed beyond the comprehension of mind and spirit; I felt jarred in the depths of my soul. I was witnessing the effects of a horror too terrible to imagine. Never would I be the same again; the shock to my conscience registered permanently within me." The bomb killed an estimated 78,150 people immediately, and severely wounded 13,983.

He also witnessed the "anguished suffering of the Vietnamese ... under France's colonial imperialistic posture which the U.S. still pursued two decades later." He became convinced the world's people needed to see themselves as brothers and sisters and find an alternative to war for solving problems.

"Fundamentally, the roots of my response were spiritual," Hatfield wrote. "As best I could, I followed the beckoning to seek God's will. A unique inner abandonment flowed from heeding what my heart sensed to be truth; the consequences faded into irrelevancy."

But there were consequences of his unpopular stance against U.S. involvement in Vietnam. For many people today, it's hard to imagine that opposition to America's Southeast Asian policies in the sixties was not more widespread. History books, films, and music tend to focus on the groundswell of dissent at that time. This wasn't always true, however. When American mothers and fathers sent their sons to fight overseas and watched them die on nightly television, the need to believe that it was for a "just cause" was powerful. It was unsettling to hear an American senator suggest the war was wrong.

As Hatfield says:

> What resulted seemed pragmatically senseless and politically disastrous. Such often is the way of faith. Naturally, I sought the love and encouragement of others whose allegiance belonged to the same Lord. That is why the spiritual rejection which emanated from many quarters of the evangelical community was so devastating. When my convictions alienated me from the Christian community I felt called to serve, I began to reconsider my calling to the political vocation.

Then a simple but significant act from graduate students gave Hatfield the courage to continue and demonstrated that "some fellow evangelicals were understanding the implications of the Gospel in radically new ways." The event occurred in June of 1970, during the national convulsions following the invasion of Cambodia two months earlier and the killing of unarmed students at Kent State by the National Guard.

President Dave Hubbard asked him to give the commencement address at Fuller Theological Seminary in Pasadena, which left Hatfield with mixed emotions:

> I was at a total loss to know how to relate to fellow theologically conservative Christians and was filled with considerable anxiety, not sure at all what to expect. Further, some of Fuller's conservative, wealthy supporters had made known to people at the seminary their displeasure over my appearance. Continually, it seemed as though I was becoming a divisive force within the evangelical community, a role I had no desire to play. Yet, I felt compelled to say what was on my heart, without compromising my convictions.

Having no idea how his address would be received, he was expecting the worst:

> I walked into First Methodist Church, and their enthusiastic welcome caught me quite off guard. Then, just as I was about to begin my address, students in the balcony held up

MATTERS OF THE HEART

a sign which read, "We're with you, Mark." It is difficult fully to describe all that went on within me. Somehow that one act symbolized so much that I had been longing to sense. There was an inner surge of joy, peace, and strength which I vividly recall to this day. These brothers and sisters were really with me; their acceptance created a sense of spiritual solidarity which I had rarely experienced from any segments within the Church.

As the students came forward to receive degrees, he was stunned to see that almost two-thirds of them wore black armbands in protest against the war:

Again, this simple symbolic act coming from these students had a profound effect on my heart. It demonstrated that there were countless evangelicals, who because of their faith in Christ, could not condone the immoral and barbarian violence our nation was inflicting throughout Indochina. After commencement, a letter was handed to me, a petition stating that the undersigned fully supported me as a Christian brother in my effort to halt our involvement in Indochina, and specially endorsed the McGovern-Hatfield Amendment to cut off funds for the War.

Signed by over half the faculty at Fuller, this document made Hatfield feel overwhelmed with love and acceptance. He considered this moment as one of the most significant events of that entire year, offering an initial sign of hope about the potential response among Christians to the issues of social and political concern "which I felt were critical to our witness."

In his book, he talks candidly about the complexity of living in the highest arenas of American politics while trying to live a life of conviction. Here are some excerpts of his personal quest to be a "servant leader":

———————

Power and prestige could not be the goals which gave my life a sense of direction or purpose. Those values had to be relinquished if my commitment was to be authentic. The purpose of my life is to be faithful to

Jesus Christ, to follow his way, and to be molded according to the imprint of his life.

Service to others, solely for their own behalf and even entailing deep sacrifice, is the true essence of leadership and the ultimate form of power. There is a power in servanthood which transcends all notions of power sought after so avidly in the secular political sphere of life. He or she is called to be a servant-leader. Radical allegiance to Jesus Christ transforms one's entire perspective on political reality. Priorities become totally changed; a whole new understanding of what is truly important bursts forth. There is an uncompromised identification with the needs of the poor and the oppressed. One is placed in fundamental opposition to structures of injustice and forms of national idolatry. Further, there is a commitment to the power of love as the only means to the end. We are to empty ourselves as he did for the sake of others.

If humanity is to emerge with any promise into the next century, we must unlock all our spiritual resources. Without them, I believe that we will either destroy ourselves, or be destroyed by our hatreds and greeds.

Old Jewish proverb: "God gives you the task. He does not ask that you succeed, but he does ask that you not lay it aside."◘

Ecology
and Theology:
A Natural Linkage ▣

Glance at the sun. See the moon and the stars.
Gaze at the beauty of earth's greenings.
Now, think.
What delight God gives to humankind
with all these things . . .
All nature is at the disposal of humankind.
We are to work with it. For
without it we cannot survive.

HILDEGARD OF BINGEN

The earth does not belong to people; people belong to the
earth. . . . This earth is precious to the Creator and to
harm the earth is to heap contempt upon its Creator.

CHIEF SEATTLE

Chief Seattle's words of concern and wisdom were
spoken over a hundred years ago at a time when he could only
have guessed at the devastation humans would cause the earth in
the twentieth century. But he understood in his heart what many
church leaders are suggesting today: The environmental crisis is
not just a biological, economic, or political issue—it's a moral and
spiritual one as well.

Though belatedly, churches worldwide are now beginning to
understand the essential link between theology and ecology. If we
love our Creator, we must cherish the created earth, our planet
home. It is God's gift to us. It is, as Native Americans figuratively
say, our mother. There's power in this metaphor because it implies
a deep bond of love, and yet people pour chemicals into the
bloodstream of this mother; they turn away when they see her

ancient limbs amputated; they burn down her fertile backyard for quick profits and drown her in non-biodegradable garbage. We would grieve to see a loved one so abused. If our own mother were threatened, wouldn't we do everything we could to bring our family and friends together to rescue and heal her?

Some are trying. Many in the secular world have devoted great energy to these concerns, but they are finding themselves burning out in despair and hopelessness. It is an important issue to many college students, demonstrated by their support of an environmental conference in Illinois in the fall of 1990, which drew 7000 students instead of the predicted 2000.

Around the same time, Christians gathered in Seattle with people from other faith traditions in a "Earth and Spirit" conference. Participants from over thirty-eight states and many nations came together to think about the link between our theology and ecology. Co-sponsored by the Chinook Learning Community on Whidbey Island and the Cathedral of St. John the Divine in New York City, the three-day workshop included presentations that will be published for the 1992 United Nations conference on the environment in Brazil. "There's no Buddhist sun, Hindu moon, or Christian river," said the Rev. Fritz Hull, co-director, with his wife, Vivian, of Chinook. "Together, we all need to look at what our religious traditions teach us about loving the planet and share this vision."

For many years, the church has been silent on ecological matters, perhaps out of a fear of pantheism—the belief that nature itself is God. But it has not always been so. Many of the spiritual writers of earlier centuries found the beauty of the natural world to be a strong source of understanding the Creator.

One such person was Hildegard of Bingen. She lived more than eight hundred years ago in the lush Rhineland valley of Germany. A remarkable Renaissance personality, she established a monastery, composed joyful music, painted, taught, and wrote extensively in the fields of science, ethics, medicine, and theology.

Educated in the male-dominated Benedictine tradition of the time, she repressed much of her brilliant talent for many years. This conflict led to a four-year illness. During this period she received visions from God, which included a clear sense of direction that she should write. As she obeyed and began writing the book *Know the Ways,* she found herself fully healed. Many of her illuminations focus on our relationship with the earth and provide a fertile field of study for Christians interested in environmental issues. She once wrote, "The Word is living, being, spirit, all verdant greening, all creativity. This Word manifests itself in every creature."

In describing the nature of God she writes:

> *I am the breeze that nurtures all things green.*
> *I encourage blossoms to flourish with ripening fruits.*
> *I am the rain coming from the dew*
> *that causes the grasses to laugh*
> *with the joy of life.*

Another early voice who celebrated the connections between God, the earth, and all God's creatures was St. Francis of Assisi. Look at the opening lines of his "Canticle of the Creatures":

> *All praise be yours, my Lord, through Sisters Moon and Stars;*
> *All praise be yours, my Lord, through Brothers Wind and Air;*
> *All praise be yours, my Lord, through Sister Water . . .*

Such Christian thinkers as these, along with many contemporaries like Sean McDonagh (who wrote *To Care for the Earth: A Call to a New Theology*), Teilhard de Chardin, a Jesuit philosopher, Matthew Fox in his book *Original Blessing: A Primer in Creation Spirituality,* or Annie Dillard, offer thoughtful reflections on our earth home.

Have you considered the connection between your faith and your concerns for our planet? They aren't separate. Why not start a study-action group and read thinkers who are wrestling with these issues. Or go to the Bible, especially the Psalms, and see what it says about cherishing the created world. A scarred mother needs an infusion of your healing energy.▣

Seoul on Sunday: A Traveler's Peace ◙

The peace of God, which transcends all understanding, will guard your hearts and your minds in Christ Jesus.

PHILIPPIANS 4:7

"Oh, you young people—why would you ever want to go to Latin America?"

WOMAN TALKING TO STUDENTS ON THEIR WAY TO GUATEMALA

Are you ever nervous just before traveling? Whether you are flying great distances, driving home with friends, or going to a foreign country, it's not uncommon to be concerned about safety.

Nor does it just happen to students. One time a Fulbright professor needed to travel to Asia with his wife and two children during a time of anxiety about terrorist attacks. "It was an unsettling time, and our families were especially nervous," he admitted, "but it was a wonderful opportunity."

Shortly after their long uncomfortable flight, they arrived in Seoul on a Sunday morning and decided to attend a Korean church service. The church's pastor read the words from Psalm 139, which have reassured travelers for centuries:

> *Where can I go from your Spirit?* ...
> *If I rise on the wings of the dawn,*
> *if I settle on the far side of the sea,*
> *even there your hand will guide me,*
> *your right hand will hold me fast.*

"It was such an affirmation," recalled the professor's wife. "We'd literally been on 'the wings of the dawn,' arriving as the sun rose in the morning."

MATTERS OF THE HEART

Later that evening, they rode the train to their new home in Taegu. All along the way, red neon crosses illuminated the village churches. The professor's wife said, "You had a sense if you were ever lost, you could find your way to a church. We started our travels with an abiding sense that wherever we are—no matter how far from the security of home—God is there."

In the Bible, story after story describes God's people as sojourners in this world. Leaving home was part of the challenge confronting many men and women in the Old and New Testaments. Abraham, Sarah, Moses, Hannah, and Ruth all left the security of their known world to follow God. Mary and Joseph not only traveled the crowded road toward Bethlehem, but also the lonely road away from it when they fled with the newborn Jesus into Egypt. He began life as a refugee!

When Jesus started his public ministry, he walked the dusty roads from town to town. The disciples left their familiar jobs and homes to answer his call to "follow me." Paul ventured throughout the Mediterranean to spread the Good News.

Nor were these Club Med vacations—travel for rest and relaxation. All of God's people encounter hardships and experience famine, shipwreck, loneliness, persecution, jail, and even death; but still their stories exude joy and confidence because they trust the promise that God is with them.

Traveling stretches our faith. Inevitably, it rattles our secure ways of being and offers different perspectives on life—and often leads us to depend more on God than on family, friends, or even ourselves.

John, a freshman from Seattle enrolled at Georgetown University in Washington, D.C., remembers making this startling discovery. Having grown up in Seattle, surrounded by a loving Catholic family and being a superstar in his high school, he felt extremely confident as he took off for a college 2,500 miles away. "I couldn't understand why my family fussed so much at my leaving—I could hardly wait to get away."

But when John landed at Chicago's O'Hare Airport and walked into the airport lobby packed with thousands of strangers, an overwhelming sense of aloneness engulfed him. To his surprise, he started to cry. "I've never told my folks this, but realizing no one there knew me or cared about me knocked out my pride real fast." He also credits that moment as giving him a new appreciation of his exceptional family life and religious heritage.

Do you travel with trust? Or do you allow your fears to keep you from venturing into the unknown? We live in an era when, within hours, we can mingle with people who are vastly different from us—brothers and sisters we could never have met a century ago. If you believe in the psalmist's assurance that God's "right hand will hold me fast" wherever you go, why not say yes to the great mandate to "go into all the world"? ◘

Mood Swings
and Creativity ◉

The people walking in darkness have seen a great light.

ISAIAH 9:2

It is tempting to assume that creativity comes to people when they are feeling good, not when they are low. Yet the demands of college to learn, write, think, and create never cease— no matter what your mood. One essential skill for college survival is the refusal to let moods dictate actions. Any musician, artist, or writer has learned that if we quit when we don't feel like working, we may forfeit some of our best work.

George Frideric Handel learned this when he wrote one of the world's most jubilant pieces of music, the *Messiah*. Each Christmas, Christians around the world find their spirits inspired with comfort and praise as they stand and join in singing the famous "Hallelujah Chorus"—especially the words "Wonderful, Counselor, the Mighty God, the Everlasting Father, the Prince of Peace."

You would think that Handel must have been in an exceptionally spiritual state of mind to write his masterpiece, but the truth is, his creation was born in deep discouragement. Although famed as a musician, on a certain evening in 1741, Handel was wandering the dark streets of London in despair, seeking to avoid his many creditors. The frigid winter had closed England's theaters, and after the death of Queen Caroline, Handel's staunch patronness, he found himself deeply in debt.

Four years earlier, he had survived a paralyzing stroke. Now, bent on his cane, the fifty-six-year-old Handel cried out to God: "Why did you permit my resurrection only to allow my fellow men to bury me again? My God, why hast thou forsaken me?"

Wearily, he returned to his lodgings on Brook Street, climbed the stairs, and noticed a bulky parcel on his desk. Inside was a libretto entitled "A Sacred Oratorio" from a friend who wanted Handel to compose the music. Handel wasn't interested in religious composition and, snuffing out his candle, went to bed. But unable to sleep, he arose to glance at the manuscript.

Turning the pages, he discovered, "The people that walk in darkness . . ." and then, "His name shall be called Wonderful, Counselor . . ." Entranced, he read on. Then for the next twenty-four days, almost without food or rest, Handel feverishly composed the now-famous *Messiah*. He afterward said, "I did think I did see all Heaven before me, and the great God himself!"

When the 275-page manuscript was completed, Handel found himself no longer depressed, and with the money he made on the composition, he was able to pay off his creditors. When he first performed the work in Dublin, he insisted that the profits go to charity, especially to the relief of prisoners in several jails. "I do not want to make money out of this work for which I am indebted to Another."

Daniel, a twenty-one-year-old California student with a passion for music, doesn't pretend to be Handel (yet), but he experienced a similar amazement at being able to create while "not in the mood." He had been working on a musical for three weeks, lyric after lyric and note after note. In his journal he wrote, "I was really worn down, felt empty, and had no more words to write. I stopped to take a break, and leaving the music studio, I walked down to the coffee room and sat on a soft green couch. It would have been so easy to just fall into a deep sleep right there. But I couldn't. I needed to write this song now."

The name of the musical was *Moses,* and Danial was scheduled to start recording it in Burbank at 10:00 A.M. the following Saturday. "I'd been writing since 11:00 Friday morning, and now it was 1:35 A.M. I had to get this last piece done for the recording session, which was a one-shot deal. After Saturday it would be another eight months before we could use the facilities at Warner Bros. Studio again."

In near panic, he left the studio and stopped at his home church. "I was desperate, searching the depths of my mind for

MATTERS OF THE HEART

anything that would make sense." He walked into the sanctuary and sat at the piano, hoping the setting might inspire him. "I began plucking the keys of the piano, but nothing but disharmonies came forth. I banged on the piano with my fists and folded my arms as I dropped my head on them.

"I was angry and doubted myself and my musical abilities. Then I remembered what it was I needed to write about. The words had to reflect Moses' feelings after he found the Jews worshiping idols and getting drunk. He was angry and doubted his ability to lead God's people. The words began to flow as did the melody."

That morning Daniel met the recording deadline and sang his new song, called "Who Am I?" When the musical toured, it turned out to be most people's favorite—and his as well. "This helped me see that all emotions, even negative ones, can be turned into good."

Do you let your emotions control you? The Bible promises that if we ask for help, with God's power we will do "exceedingly abundant" . . . or "immeasurably more . . . than all that we ask or imagine" (Ephesians 3:20). Handel experienced this great truth— a tired, discouraged old man who created a musical masterpiece. Daniel discovered this—a tired, discouraged young man who wrote a musical that is still being sung in local churches. Whether it's preparing for a test, writing an essay, working in a science lab, or practicing a speech, don't wait for positive emotions before beginning the task. Creativity comes to the person who acts.▣

Acts of Trust ▣

It seems crazy that the God of the Universe could care about the daily details of our lives. But maybe that's the ultimate test of faith. A NINETEEN-YEAR-OLD WOMAN

Trust is an elusive word in a troubled age like ours. We are invited to place our trust in God's loving care. But painful experiences can seal shut the deepest recesses of many people's hearts. For those who want God to shape their lives, learning to open those sealed doors can be a major challenge.

Trust is often mistaken for passivity. People often think that trust is a kind of "God will take care of everything" mentality, demanding no willingness on our part to be God's hands and feet.

Best-selling author Catherine Marshall, in her book *Beyond Ourselves,* wrote a candid account of her first efforts at practicing the right kind of trust. When she was a senior in high school, she explained, she was confronted with the problem of financing a college education.

For Catherine, the daughter of a minister in a poor railroad town in West Virginia during the Depression, lack of money was an everyday reality. She was a fine student and dreamed of a college education, but at that time the government didn't offer loans to deserving students.

So on faith, Catherine applied for a scholarship. She was accepted at Agnes Scott College in Decatur, Georgia, and was given a small work-study scholarship, to which she added 125 dollars she had saved from high-school essay and debating prizes. But she was still several hundred dollars short.

She describes the night her mother introduced her to how practical trust works:

> My mother said quietly, "You and I are going to pray about this.... But let's talk about this a minute before we

pray. . . . I believe that it is God's will for you to go to college, or else He would not have given you the mental equipment. Furthermore, all resources are at God's disposal. Do you believe that, Catherine?"

"Yes—yes—I think I do."

"All right. Now here's another fact I want you to think about. Everybody has faith. We're born with it. Much of what happens to us in life depends on where we place our faith. If we deposit it in God, then we're on sure ground. If we place our trust in poverty or failure or fear, then we're investing it poorly. So keep that in mind while I read something to you." She opened a Moffatt Bible to 1 John 5:14–15:

Now the confidence we have in him is this,
that he listens to us whenever we ask anything
in accordance with his will; and if we know that he
listens to whatever we ask, we know that we obtain the
requests we have made to him.

"Note how the thought goes in that promise, Catherine. Whenever we ask God for something that is His will, He hears us. If He hears us, then He grants the request we have made. So you and I can rest on that promise. Let's claim it right now for the resources for your college." And so we knelt by the bed and prayed about it.

During those quiet moments in the bedroom, I was learning what faith is and how it works. It is true that my faith was immature and weak, but the strength of Mother's was contagious. She had helped me take my first step in faith. The answer would come. We knew it would, though neither of us had any idea how.

For Catherine, it came when her mother was offered the job—through the Federal Writers' Project—of writing the history of their county. It paid enough for Catherine's college expenses. She wrote, "That was the way I learned that we must have faith before the fact, not after, if we are to function as human beings at all. The only question is—faith in whom? Faith in what?"

I hesitate to relate this story because I don't want to present God as a kind of Santa Claus—a spiritual gift-giver who gives us whatever *we* think is best for us. But like most honest stories of spiritual struggle, Catherine Marshall's shows how she faced a genuine difficulty in trust.

If you look carefully at her story, you see that she wasn't passive. She had given her full effort to the available options for college-minded students at the time; she entered debate and writing contests, saved her earnings, applied for scholarships. But it wasn't enough; she had to depend on the One with infinite resources.

Because higher education today, especially at private institutions, is so expensive, students struggle with financing their dream. Those who trust God most in this are also often the ones who fill out many scholarship applications, look for part-time jobs, or even drop out a semester to earn money. Answers to prayer may come in ways that require new flexibility—like the students at Oregon State University who get free housing and food if they serve in the local fire station.

Is it hard for you to trust God? If not in the financial arena, perhaps in friendships? In romance? In career choice? In moral choices? Jesus said, "Everything is possible for him who believes" (Mark 9:23). But trust takes practice. Why not entrust God with in one hard area of your life and begin the practice of active faith now? ▣

An Easter
Meditation ▣

When I started reading the Bible through the eyes of the poor, passages took on completely new meanings. Try it— it's amazing! SOCIOLOGY PROFESSOR DON LIEBERT

One of the skills developed in college is critical thinking, which includes trying to see something from another person's point of view, or as a Native American proverb says: Don't judge others until "you've walked a mile in their moccasins."

If you were to study in Latin America, for example, you would hear a lot about liberation theology, a common approach to theology where oppression exists. At its core, this perspective emphasizes that the biblical account demonstrates God's unwavering commitment to the poor. To help Christians who live in abundance understand this, Peruvian theologian Gustavo Gutierrez encourages "changing our lenses" and try reading biblical stories from the viewpoint of society's disadvantaged. Actually, reading the Bible from many different angles is an excellent way of getting past our preconceived perspectives.

I thought of this recently while reading the Bible's account of the hours surrounding Christ's crucifixion. Only, this time I tried to imagine what this story might mean to one of the many political prisoners throughout the world who endure torture, abandonment, shame, and death because of their faith. Some historians say that the twentieth century has actually produced more martyrs than any other known period. Some are famous, like Oscar Romero or the nuns murdered in El Salvador. Others are unknown, like the peasants killed at Lake Atitlan, Guatemala, or the Christians in Uganda. Many are ordinary citizens who risk danger by taking an active part in a church community.

What helped me imagine their plight was meeting one such political prisoner, Camillo Cortez. A Chilean engineer and Methodist lay pastor working with the poor in his country, on September 11, 1973, he was one of many people to be arrested during Pinochet's military coup, which toppled the Allende regime. Camillo spent twenty-one torturous months in prison. His worst anguish was being forced to watch as interrogators threw his youngest son from a second-floor window in a desperate attempt to persuade Cortez to confess to crimes he had never committed.

The constant torture, the extreme loneliness, and the cries of other prisoners left him weak and almost beyond hope. One time, Cortez and a Catholic priest decided to ask the guards to let them hold a Sunday communion service in an attempt to give comfort to the other men. To their surprise, the guards agreed, found some old bread and cheap wine, and herded the hundreds of men into a large outdoor sunken field. Guards circled the area from above, aiming loaded guns at the battered and bruised victims of violence.

"Was this going to be a mass slaughter?" wondered Cortez. Ignoring the guns, Cortez and his friend offered the ancient words of celebration of Christ's suffering love as they gave the bread and wine to each man. "Here is my body—broken for you; here is my blood—shed for you."

For Cortez the reenactment of this common ceremony intensified his own sense of God's great mercy. "For these men, who had not known a touch of kindness for months, the gratefulness in their eyes taught me how important small acts of faith are. Like Christ, they knew first hand what it meant to suffer broken and bloody bodies for crimes they hadn't committed. And shame, abandonment, aloneness. We identified in new ways with Christ's costly gift—given so that we might live lives close to God. In his innocence, he endured the torture unto death for us."

After this experience, Cortez decided to serve Christ in prison by helping the other prisoners in every way feasible, and he felt new courage to endure until death if needed.

Unlike others, Cortez didn't die—in fact, he feels a kind of resurrection. Because of the work of Amnesty International, a nonpartisan organization from London that works for the release of nonviolent political prisoners, authorities eventually released him, flying him to exile in America. He then moved with his wife to the East Coast serving a Spanish speaking congregation. Word of his exceptional kindness to other prisoners filtered out and earned him a national humanitarian award. And his son survived and escaped to Sweden.

When Cortez spoke on our campus, what most struck students was his lack of bitterness after experiencing such atrocities. He exudes a surprising spirit of forgiveness and hope, living out Christ's words on the cross, "Forgive them, Father, for they know not what they do." Cortez now channels his efforts into helping other political prisoners through Amnesty's local chapters, many on college campuses.

Why not try reading the Word by coming at it intentionally from another angle? Perhaps trying to see it through the eyes of someone you know or through a character in the story? There are many contemporary biblical scholars who are writing books to help us approach the Word with freshness, such as African-American writer Renita J. Weems. Her book, *Just a Sister Away,* written to be used as a study guide for small groups, reconstructs the relationships between women in the Bible in a creative way.

"The Word of God is living and active. Sharper than any double-edged sword" (Hebrews 4:12). If it has become dull for you because of always reading it in the traditional way—asking, "What does this say to me?"—then try reading in an innovative way. Ask, rather, "What does this say to my neighbor?" Walking through the Bible in another person's moccasins might be an important step in becoming a compassionate neighbor.◙

MATTERS
OF
THE
SOUL

Introduction:
The Interior Life ◉

My soul thirsts for God, for the living God.   PSALM 42:2

Each of us possesses a soul, but we do not prize our souls as creatures made in God's image deserve and so we do not understand the great secrets that they contain.
ST. TERESA OF AVILA

Doubts are the messengers of the Living One to the honest.
GEORGE MACDONALD

Living a life of adventuresome faith on a college campus takes a certain spirit of *intention*. Almost inevitably, for most thoughtful students, college provides a time to ask questions and express doubts about what they have learned from others about God.

It is important in such times to think of faith not as a noun, but a verb—active, not static. It can't be lost because of an honest heart and mind. Writer Frederick Buechner, in an address he gave at Yale, later published as *Wishful Thinking: A Theological ABC,* talks about the role of faith and doubt. In it he states, "Whether your faith is that there is a God or that there is not a God, if you don't have any doubts you are either kidding yourself or asleep. Doubts are the ants in the pants of faith. They keep it awake and moving."

For some students, wrestling with emotional or intellectual questions about their faith creates fear and confusion. Afraid of losing their faith if they explore these nudges to their hearts and minds, they may grow intellectually and socially but stay spiritually stunted. By the time they graduate, it seems like they are entering the adult world with a leather briefcase of college skills in one hand and a child's Snoopy lunchbox of spiritual understanding in the other. They have never allowed themselves to discover the magnificence of the God of the universe.

Other students embrace the truth that "God has not given us the spirit of fear, but of power, and of love, and of a sound mind" (2 Timothy 1:7, King James Version). They see college as the perfect time to explore all the truths of God—and they instinctively know that the God who created the majesty of the Rocky Mountains, the intricacies of the human body, and the boundless emotional range of human nature, certainly must welcome our genuine questions. In fact, they act this out in their lives, often emerging as leading Christian scientists, artists, philosophers, dancers, teachers, government leaders, living out the call to "love the Lord your God with all your heart and with all your soul and with all your mind" (Matthew 22:37). But this takes time and attention. It rarely just happens.

Author E. B. White once wrote a Christmas story that sounds a lot like the challenge of discovering a vital faith during college. He tells of being a little boy and going to a local sporting-goods store a few days before Christmas. There he found a fascinating trumpetlike device that hunters hold to their ears. If they listen carefully, they can hear the distant music of the hounds. He suggests this is what we all need during our commercialized Christmases when the materialism that surrounds Christ's birth makes it hard to hear God's genuine story. White believes the contemporary miracle is that no amount of canned musical "Silent Nights" in the shopping malls or abundance of Santa Clauses or cheap tinsel has been able to dim the 2000-year-old message that still penetrates human hearts. It can't be destroyed. But one has to listen carefully—like the hunters—to hear the music of Christ's birth.

The faith life of some college students resembles this. With the daily demands of exams, papers, readings, jobs, friendships, or money worries, it is easy not to take time to listen to the voice of God in one's life. "I found I put my faith on hold for a year," explains a college sophomore, now very much wanting to place the trumpet to his ear. He senses these are important years—the time he will most likely choose a vocation, make life-long friends, perhaps even meet a future wife. Although student styles are

MATTERS OF THE SOUL

different, they attest to the need to carve out time in their days or week for meditation, study, and prayer.

They have discovered a truth similar to the hunters. If one listens very carefully, one will hear the distant music of the Lord. "To love the Lord with all one's soul" draws students to create times for quiet conversation, to not let the noise of campus life drown out their interior life.

One twentieth-century Christian who understood spiritual struggle and the absolute need to find moments of quiet was Dag Hammarskjöld, the Swedish diplomat who became the highly respected Secretary-General of the United Nations. After his death in a plane crash en route to negotiations in Africa, his journal was found, in which he related his own quest for a living faith in the midst of demanding days. For long periods of time he fought feelings of despair and loneliness, the "dark night of the soul" that the Spanish poet and theologian St. John of the Cross describes so eloquently. Hammarskjöld jotted down his battle: "To preserve the silence within . . . amid all the noise. To remain open and quiet."

In his journal, later published under the title of *Markings,* Hammarskjöld wrote of the difference in our lives when we live in a relationship with our Creator. "God does not die on the day when we cease to believe in a personal deity, but we die on the day when our lives cease to be illumined by the steady radiance, renewed daily, of a wonder, the source of which is beyond all reason." As Hammarskjöld stated, we can choose to live our daily lives touched by the radiance of God.

Besides taking time for this relationship, college students often find that seeking out other Christians is also pivotal for spiritual growth. But it isn't always easy.

Usually, a person's first understanding of God and the Christian life has come through others. Often it begins in the family or in a specific faith community like their home church or a para-church organization. Even at a Christian college, students come from a variety of backgrounds: Baptists meet Episcopalians; Catholics meet Pentacostals; Presbyterians, Lutherans, and Methodists meet independent church students.

At first, some students find it hard to give up the idea that "my way" is better. Trying to find others with identical belief systems can be impossible—and inevitably limiting. "I was angry at the chaplain's office my whole freshman year," recalls one student, "because I was sure they weren't doing things 'right.' Finally, I realized they just weren't approaching students the way my high-school youth leader did."

Actually, if you're fortunate, there may be a campus fellowship where you can gather with other Christians and stretch your faith. But beware of cliques or Christian ghettos—a common occurrence especially on secular university campuses. God doesn't call us to comfortable isolation.

Also, because on-campus groups primarily involve young adults, they inevitably have limitations. "When you spend all your time with twenty-year-olds, you begin to go nuts!" explained one senior, who had found being with little children and adults in a local church a very important change each week.

As St. Teresa of Avila suggests, if we do not prize our souls as creatures made in God's image deserve, we may miss the great secrets they contain! Taking time for the interior life, both alone and in the community of God's people promises to bring us closer to our Creator. It's worthy of our best energies. "For what will it profit them if they gain the whole world but forfeit their life?" (Matthew 16:26, *New Revised Standard Version*). ◙

When Your
World Turns ◫

*Surely goodness and love will follow me all the days of
my life.*   PSALM 23:6

A question on many scholarship applications reads:
"What are your short-term and long-term goals?"

"This question always frustrates me," said Debbie, an
exceptional international-studies student who actually enjoys goal
setting. "I can tell them I want to maintain my 3.7 grade point
without letting grades control my life, that I've applied for a
semester in Washington, D.C., to work in a Christian-studies
program in politics, and that I plan to go on to grad school. But
how do I talk about my growing openness to God's direction that
may reveal other options? Or my belief that God steers a moving
ship?"

Debbie wisely understands the creative, lifelong tension
Christians face trying to balance responsible planning and being
open to divine interruptions. And she seems to have the humble
awareness that we can't always control our lives. Openness to God
is no easy task, especially in our cultural climate of "success
planning," which assumes we're always directors of our own
destiny.

Dom Helder Camara, the Brazilian archbishop, speaks to one
side of this tension in his book of poems, *A Thousand Reasons for
Living.* Camara spends his days working with the poor in Recife
and has twice been nominated for a Nobel Peace Prize for his
compassionate, committed ministry. He spends many nights
writing, rising at 2:00 A.M. to listen to the voices so frequently
drowned out by the daytime noise. It is then, he says, that "God

talks to me, nature too, and the human heart." If a serendipity or serious surprise causes your life to take a turn, he suggests

> *Accept*
> *surprises*
> *that upset your plans*
> *shatter your dreams*
> *give a completely*
> *different turn*
> *to your day*
> *and—who knows?—*
> *to your life*
> *It is not chance*
> *Leave the Father free*
> *himself to weave*
> *the patterns of your days*

Are you upset if everything doesn't go perfectly as planned? Has there been a surprise in your life that invites you to trust God's loving hand? This is rarely easy at first. But many times in our lives we may be living out what we perceive to be our "second choices." You may have experienced this if you've ever been rejected by your number-one college choice, or preferred sorority, fraternity, or roommates, or didn't get into your desired classes, or lost a friendship.

What a difference it makes when we approach these disappointments with a trust in the Divine Weaver, rather than an insistence on our Divine Rights.◙

Who's in Control? ▣

There are plenty who follow our Lord halfway, but not the other half. They will give up possessions, friends, and honors, but it touches them too closely to disown themselves. MEDIEVAL MYSTIC MEISTER ECKHART

God wants more: he lays claim not to half the will, but the whole.... He wants not only the good fruits, but the whole tree; not only action, but being; not something, but myself—and myself wholly and entirely.
GERMAN THEOLOGIAN HANS KÜNG

Giving up our will to God's is never a one-time act but an on-going, often daily, act of trust. In many ways our culture encourages us to be closed, tight, independent people. From the two-year-old's insistence, "I do it myself," to Frank Sinatra's proud theme song, "I Did It My Way," we're urged to be the proud directors of our destinies.

It's understandable, then, why it's easy to be lukewarm, to be Christians of convenience, only letting God into those parts of our lives we choose to open and keeping closed the doors to our private rooms: "Lord, you can help me shape my present friendships, but stay out of my past hurts," or "Direct my job search, but don't detour my goals."

Students understand how emotions sabotage them. One female student, struggling with a sense of distance from God, said, "I often rely on my feelings as my barometer of faith, rather than trusting in the fact of God's love."

There are nine words of Jesus, a cry of the heart before the crucifixion, that show his spirit of total self-surrender. In his most difficult moment, he chose to trust the Divine design, not his feelings: "Not my will, however, but your will be done" (Luke

22:42, *Good News Bible*). In those words, he found the ultimate resting place of the soul.

In reading spiritual biographies, I often see this human tendency to let our feelings dictate our faith. In her book *Beyond Ourselves,* Catherine Marshall insists, "Feelings are at the bottom of most of our Christian difficulties." In one chapter, "The Secret of the Will," she tells of discovering earlier writers like Quaker Hannah Whitall Smith, whose classic *Christian's Secret of a Happy Life,* sold almost three million copies early in this century. Smith in turn traced her discovery of this secret to a seventeenth-century French writer, François Fénelon, a cleric with extraordinary insight into human nature.

The secret, as Catherine Marshall states it, is simply this:

> That the Christian life must be lived in the will, not in the emotions; that God regards the decisions and choices of the man himself, no matter how contrary his emotions may be. . . . The dictionary describes will as "the power of conscious deliberate action." Before God, we're only responsible for the act of that will.

The Bible urges us to let the Wonderful Counselor radiate into all areas of our lives—every corner. In this lies the adventure. "Those who love me will keep my word, and my Father will love them, and we will come to them and make our home with them." Then Jesus adds, "Whoever does not love me does not keep my words" (John 14:23, *New Revised Standard Version*).

The God of the Universe wants to make a home—a dwelling place—within us. And with this follows the promise, "I have told you this so that my joy may be in you and that your joy may be complete" (John 15:11). As Hans Küng wrote, "Jesus' call to conversion is a call to joy. . . . This then is God's will: man's well-being."

What does this mean in our daily lives? "Those who love me will keep my word" makes clear that faith is only real when obedience is present. One of the first acts of faith involves becoming "people of the book," reading carefully our sacred Scriptures so we know the Word. To neglect it inevitably means we refuse to know the Giver. Many colleges offer courses in Old and New Testament, an excellent way to deepen one's intellectual foundations of faith.

Fortunately, holy obedience concerns the will, not the emotions. When C. S. Lewis describes his unemotional commitment to God, he tells of two external changes he decided to make. First, he started going to church (which he disliked at first), because he believed Christians are called to community. Second, he started reading the Bible, an act he continued almost every day of his life. Or consider the example of Bill. Shy by nature, he started telling members of his family, "I love you," even though it felt awkward at first. He acted, despite his feelings. Joan, raised in a pentecostal church, often doubted her relationship with God whenever her feelings of closeness waivered. To get beyond the feeling factor, she memorized verses that assured her of her relationship to God, like Isaiah 43:1, 3: "Fear not; for I am with you ... I have called you by your name, you are mine."

"Every moment and every situation challenges us to action and obedience. ... We must get into action and obey," insists Dietrich Bonhoeffer in his book *The Cost of Discipleship*. Or in the words of Thomas Kelly, the Quaker author of *The Testament of Devotion*:

> Begin where you are. Obey now. Use what little obedience you are capable of, even if it be like a grain of mustard seed. Begin where you are ... in the deeper levels of your lives where you are all alone with God the Loving Eternal One, keep up a silent prayer, "Open thou my life. Guide my thoughts where I dare not let them go. But Thou darest. Thy will be done."

Jeff, a sophomore, decided to act on this call to obedience in a previously neglected area of his life. "I knew that God wants us to give part of our money to the church to help others, but I was usually broke." A financial-aid student, he earned about a hundred dollars a month through work-study. "I always had excuses, like, 'I'm not financially stable,' or 'I don't have a home church.' But then last summer, I started thinking, 'Why wait?' After all, who knows when I'll ever be financially stable or have a home church? So every month I started giving a portion of my money to the college church I attend. I had to start sometime. If I say I want God in all of my life, this has to include economics."

Is there an area of your life where an act of obedience could reflect a desire to follow and trust God's will, instead of insisting on you own? Do your feelings get in the way of obeying that "still small voice"? Try acting on the "secret of the will" and obey God's Word, regardless of the emotions of the moment. If we welcome God into all the rooms of our heart, we are promised a home where joy enters.◙

The Confessions
of St. Augustine ◙

Oh Lord, make me chaste, but not yet.   ST. AUGUSTINE

Man can live on forgiveness.
                        GERMAN THEOLOGIAN HANS KÜNG

Do you tend to put religious leaders on pedestals, thinking they never wrestle with the same temptations common to the rest of us? If you take any Western civilization courses, you'll encounter Saint Augustine, the fourth-century North African who profoundly shaped the early Christian church and medieval religious thought. His ideas eventually influenced Immanuel Kant, Blaise Pascal, John Calvin, Martin Luther, and other church reformers.

Because of his influence, it's easy to think he always had it together—a devout and intelligent Christian philosopher and church leader. Not true! In his *Confessions,* a kind of spiritual biography that has fascinated readers through the centuries, he writes honestly of the immense struggles in his life between the ages of eighteen and thirty-one. The son of a devout Christian mother and a pagan father, Augustine pursued worldly success as a young man, became attracted to several non-Christian movements, lived with a woman from age nineteen, bore a son out of wedlock—and worried his mother, Monica, immensely.

But no amount of pleasure satisfied his restless heart. In *The Confessions,* he shows his spiritual battles in great detail—especially his battles with his strong will and lust—and his sense of God's constant guiding and pursuing love nevertheless. He recounts the afternoon in a friend's garden, while sitting under a fig tree, when he finally yielded his heart to God. He wrote, "I understood by my own experience, what I had read, how 'the flesh lusteth against the spirit and the spirit against the flesh.'" Giving full vent to his tears, he prayed:

And Thou, O Lord, how long: How long wilt Thou be angry for ever. Remember not our former iniquities, for I felt that I was held by them. How long? Tomorrow and tomorrow? Why not now? Why not is there this hour an end to my uncleanness?

At that moment, Augustine heard the voice of a child from a neighboring house chanting, "Take up and read; take up and read." "Instantly my countenance altered," he wrote. "I began to think; I arose, interpreting it to be no other than a command from God, to open the book and read the first chapter I should find."

So Augustine picked up his Bible and opened to the verse in Romans 13:13, "Not in rioting and drunkenness, not in chambering and wantonness, not in strife and envying. But put ye on the Lord Jesus Christ, and make not provision for the flesh" (King James Version). He adds that a "light of serenity infused my heart, the darkness of doubt vanished away."

Augustine finally found his heart's peace. He wrote of a joyous celebration with his mother and of his baptism, which publicly affirmed his newfound faith. Then, for over thirty-five years, he served with distinction as the Bishop of Hippo. A radical transformation!

His autobiography, in which he searches for the nature of God by looking within his own soul, was a breakthrough in literature and has served as a model for many others.

Frederick Buechner, a former chaplain at Phillips Exeter Academy, Presbyterian minister and contemporary author, also shows how we can discover in our own lives "whatever of meaning, of holiness, of God there may be to hear." In his autobiography, *The Sacred Journey,* he describes a surprising moment in college at Princeton where he first became sensitive to spiritual matters:

I was drinking beer with some friends at the Nassau
Tavern again, that scene of an earlier Epiphany, when in a
fit of tipsy anger, boredom, bravado, one of them used the
name of Jesus Christ in an oath of such blasphemy and

obscenity that it shot me out of that place like an explosion. Into the darkness of the spring night I rode my bike down Nassau Street looking for a church that was open because, even full of beer as I was, I knew I had somehow to cleanse myself, cleanse Christ, make amends somehow not just for that one boy, but for the world itself, including me, for all the lostness and sadness and ugliness of us all. Every church I came to was bolted tight at that hour, but finally I found one where, by climbing up onto a stone balustrade, I was able to at least see the lighted altar inside and clung there to the chill stone until some kind of cleansing seemed to happen, some kind of amends made, if only within myself.

Buechner would not have described himself as religious at that age, but as he reflected back on his college years he could say: "It seems to me now that a power from beyond time was working to achieve its own aim through my aimless life as it works through the lives of all of us and all our times."

Have you ever thought of looking closely at the ordinary events of your life—both painful and pleasant—to see the hand of God? As Buechner says, "Each life is not just a journey through time, but a sacred journey." Yours too! And the one common denominator we share is our invitation from Christ to join the family of forgiven people.◙

Honesty
in Little Things ▣

Tests of integrity loom before students every day. The voice of compromise will tempt you often, usually to reach some worthwhile goal. But when Christ asks that we "not conform to this world" but "be transformed," he is asking us to follow his lordship in the little things. And during the college years, the "little things" include tests, labs, essays, and research papers. The Bible refers to a far bigger test: "I know, my God, that you test the heart and are pleased with integrity" (1 Chronicles 29:17).

Apparently, cheating is on the rise on campuses, which has college officials across the country concerned. A national survey of freshmen reported that nearly 38 percent report having cheated on tests in high school, up from 30 percent the previous year. In colleges, dishonesty takes many shapes, from copying another student's homework answers or using crib sheets for a test to plagiarizing term papers.

Students try to excuse their cheating as a response to pressure: the fierce competition for top graduate schools or high-paying jobs. "These students are frightened by the job market," said Arthur Levine, chairman of the Institute for Education Management at Harvard University, in an article in the *Chronicle of Higher Education*. "They're searching for the pre-wealth curriculum. The value of money is more important to them than a code of honesty and a sense of responsibility."

Colleges are now taking steps to combat this "anything-to-succeed" attitude among students. Some are reestablishing academic honor codes abandoned in the sixties. Others have instituted an XF grade on the transcripts, showing that the student flunked for cheating. Some schools require classes in academic integrity. The University of Delaware revamped its academic code in 1985 when in a survey the university found that 78 percent of its students acknowledged their own cheating.

What difference does this make to you? Inevitably, there are times when you don't feel academically prepared. It's at those moments—often when a student is scared—that the temptation to take an easy way out appears.

But Christ speaks of the importance of being trustworthy and faithful in the small areas of our lives. It's a habit that will affect our future. "If students show a willingness to engage in academic dishonesty now, they will be more likely to engage in white-collar crime later," says Gary Pavela, the judicial-affairs officer for the University of Maryland at College Park. The newspapers abound with tales of college-educated leaders who let blind ambition corrupt their careers in law, business, politics, and government.

Our country needs a new generation of leaders characterized by integrity. When you walk across the stage to receive your diploma, will you be one? ▣

Julian of Norwich
and the Goodness
of God ◙

*She is without doubt one of the most wonderful of all
Christian voices. She gets greater and greater in my eyes as
I grow older. . . . I think that Julian of Norwich is, with
Newman, the greatest English theologian.*

THOMAS MERTON, WRITER AND TRAPPIST MONK

Have you ever watched deep-sea divers on television
bring up treasure from a ship that sank centuries ago? In 1902
scholars discovered a remarkable treasure when they found the
lost writings of a fourteenth-century English woman named
Julian, from the town of Norwich.

She lived as an anchoress, a woman who chose to live in
prayerful solitude, in a tiny apartment attached to a church.
Through one of her room's windows, which opened into the
church, she could assist at Mass and receive communion. Through
the other window, which opened outside, she received villagers
who came seeking advice and counsel. Like a good counselor
might today, she spent her days as a listening ear, hearing of pain
and loss, spiritual confusion, loneliness, from the young and old,
rich and poor.

On May 13, 1373, when Julian was thirty, she received sixteen
revelations, or "showings," of God's love in extraordinary visions.
She felt she was commanded to write them down. Several years
after that she wrote a longer version of the sixteen revelations,
showing what added insights she had received after having time
for prayer and reflection.

As a mystic, she brings her readers insights from her close encounter with a living God. Many people find her discoveries into the nature of God of great interest for our contemporary world—especially her warm affirmation of the goodness of God and creation, her personal experience with God as Mother and Father, and her confidence that God's love far surpasses our sins, that no matter what "all shall be well."

But rather than telling you more about her, here are some of her recorded thoughts:

———

On God's nature and the environment: I know well that heaven and earth and all creation are great, generous and beautiful and good ... God's goodness fills all his creatures and all his blessed works full, and endlessly overflows in them.... God is goodness ... God is nothing but goodness. God is everything which is good.

On sin: God is our friend who keeps us tenderly while we are in sin and touches us privately, showing us where we went wrong by the sweet light of compassion and grace, even though we imagine that we will be punished....

It is necessary that sin should exist. But all shall be well, and all shall be well, and all manner of thing shall be well.

For we need to fall and we need to see it; for if we did not fall, we should not know how feeble and how wretched we are in ourselves, nor too, should we know so completely the wonderful love of our Creator.

On the feminine nature of God: Just as God is truly our Father; so is God our Mother.

And so in our making, God almighty is our loving Father, and God all wisdom is our loving Mother.

But often when our falling and our wretchedness are shown to us, we are so much afraid and so greatly ashamed of ourselves that we scarcely know where we can put ourselves. But then our courteous Mother does not wish us to flee away, for nothing would be less pleasing to her; but she then wants us to behave like a child. For when it is distressed and frightened, it runs quickly to its mother; and if it can do no more, it calls to the mother for help with all its might. So she wants us to act as a meek child, saying: My kind Mother, my gracious Mother, my beloved Mother, have mercy on me.

On God's love: And with this our good Lord said most joyfully: See how I love you.◙

Facing Fear:
Martin Luther
King, Jr. ▣

*First, we must unflinchingly face our fears and honestly
ask ourselves why we are afraid. . . . Fear is mastered
through love.*   MARTIN LUTHER KING, JR.

*God has said,
"Never will I leave you;
never will I forsake you."
So we say with confidence,
"The Lord is my helper; I will not be afraid."*
                              HEBREWS 13:5–6

When we see someone act with exceptional cour-
age, it is easy to assume they are just naturally brave. As Martin
Luther King's stature grows into heroic proportions, we are in
danger of losing sight of the very human thoughts and feelings he
faced daily. Live newsreels show his public composure and bravery
as he walked the front line of direct-action marches into hostile
crowds of people and police. He confronted firehoses and vicious
dogs, billyclubs and arrest, refusing to quit even after bigots
bombed his home with his wife and infant daughter inside.

Raised in a prominent Baptist minister's home in Atlanta,
King graduated from college at nineteen and continued his
education at Crozer Theological Seminary near Philadelphia,
Pennsylvania. At heart a searcher, he read scholars and philosophers who challenged and stretched his earlier ideas about God. In
his thoughtful essay "Pilgrimage to Non-Violence," he explains
the decisions that led to his embracement of Gandhian principles
of nonviolent protest. But trying to live these out, and asking

others to follow in a land where violence dominated, tested his spirit to the core.

In the excellent biography *Let the Trumpet Sound: The Life of Martin Luther King, Jr.,* author Stephen B. Oates gives his readers a poignant glimpse into King's spiritual struggle with the "freezing and paralyzing effect of fear." During the Montgomery bus boycott, King received constant phone threats on his life, which his young wife, Coretta, often answered. He found himself wishing there might be "an honorable way out without injuring the cause." Watching Yoki, his newborn daughter, and his wife, he realized they could be taken away any moment. "I was scared to death," he admits in the 1966 interview first published in *Reflections.*

One night the phone rang. A furious, ugly voice said, "Nigger, if you aren't out of this town in three days we gonna blow your brains out and blow up your house." Then the caller hung up.

Oates writes,

> King rose and walked the floor. He thought about all the things he had studied in college, the philosophical and theological discourses on sin and evil, and realized that he couldn't take it anymore: the calls, the threats, this awful fear. He went into the kitchen and put on a pot of coffee. Yes, he had to quit; there was no other choice. He watched the coffee perk, poured a cup and sat down at the table. He brooded on how he could step down without appearing to be a coward. He thought about Coretta and Yoki and felt weak and terribly alone.

Then he heard something say to him, "You can't call on Daddy now. He's up in Atlanta a hundred and seventy-five miles away. You can't even call on Momma now."

He put his head in his hands and bowed over the table. "Oh Lord," he prayed aloud. "I'm down here trying to do what is right. But Lord, I must confess that I'm weak now. I'm afraid. The people are looking to me for leadership and if I stand before them without strength and courage, they too will falter. I am at the end of my powers. I have nothing left. I can't face it alone."

He sat there, his head still bowed in his hands, tears burning his eyes. But then he felt something—a Presence, a stirring in himself. And it seemed an inner voice was speaking to him with quiet assurance: "Martin Luther, stand up for righteousness. Stand up for justice. Stand up for truth. And lo, I will be with you, even unto the end of the world." And Oates continues, "He saw lightning flash. He heard thunder roar. It was the voice of Jesus telling him *still* to fight on. And 'he promised never to leave me, never to leave me alone. No, never alone. No, never alone. He promised never to leave me, never to leave me alone.'"

King said that when he raised his head, he felt stronger immediately. He could face the future. His trembling stopped and he felt an unusual inner calm he had never experienced before. He decided that whatever happened, God in his wisdom meant it to be. "I can stand up without fear. I can face anything." And for the first time, he found that God was profoundly real and personal to him. The idea of a personal God was no longer some "metaphysical category" that he found philosophically and theologically satisfying. No, now God was very close to him, a living God, who could transform "the fatigue of despair into the bouyancy of hope" and who would "never, ever, leave him alone."

Three days later his home was bombed, and his wife and baby barely escaped injury. But neither King, nor his family, backed down. This moment infused him with constant courage as he lead the Civil Rights Movement, which radically transformed the racial landscape of American life; it sustained him during his unpopular critique of the Vietnam War and endured to his death from an assassin's bullet at age thirty-nine.

By revealing to the world his private moment when weakness and fear consumed him, King gave God the credit for courage. "I am at the end of my powers. I have nothing left."

Toward the end of his life, he wrote:

> God has been profoundly real to me in recent years. In the midst of outer dangers I have felt an inner calm. . . . I am convinced that the universe is under the control of a loving purpose, and that in the struggle for righteousness man has cosmic companionship.

Do you ever feel at the end of your powers? Discouraged by your weak will or inability to face something? Read more of

Martin Luther King's life through any of the excellent biographies, or better yet, read his own writings. A starting place is his collection, *Strength to Love*. Also, many writing texts include samples of his essays. It is almost impossible not to draw strength from his courage.

On the other hand, if you never find anything too difficult, are the challenges you choose too small? ◙

C. S. Lewis:
The Reluctant
Convert ▣

*And so the great Angler played His fish and I never
dreamed that the hook was in my tongue.*

*Really, a young Atheist cannot guard his faith too
carefully. Dangers lie in wait for him on every side.*

C. S. LEWIS

Do you ever think people need strong emotional
experiences to commit their lives to God, that somehow a simple
act of the will isn't quite enough for God? If so, you might be
intrigued by writer C. S. Lewis's account of his gradual,
unemotional, but very real conversion.

God, in his persistence in reaching out to humans, is often
portrayed as "the hound of heaven." This image is appropriate to
Lewis's own description of his change from atheism to theism to
Christianity during his early years as a professor at Oxford
University, England. As he explained in his spiritual autobiography, *Surprised by Joy,* he considered it as ridiculous to speak of his
"search" for God as it would be to speak of the mouse's search for
the cat.

For him, faith didn't come in one moment—but in stages. At
thirty-one years of age, after spending months reading religious
writers with whom he disagreed ("They may be wrong, but
they're never boring"), he was one day riding on the top of a
British bus going up Headington Hill. He became aware of being
offered a completely free choice: either to accept or reject God.

> Without words and almost without images, a fact about
> myself was somehow presented to me. I became aware that

I was holding something at bay, or shutting something
out. . . . I felt myself being, there and then, given a free
choice. I could open the door or keep it shut. I could
unbuckle the armor or keep it on. . . . The choice appeared
to be momentous, but it was also strangely unemotional. I
was moved by no desires or fears. . . . I chose to open, to
unbuckle, to loosen the rein.

As much as Lewis understood of what he called "universal
Spirit," he opened the door. And as his life after this reveals, God
honored this faltering first step. It wasn't always pleasant,
however. "I felt as if I were a man of snow at long last beginning
to melt. The melting was starting in my back—drip-drip and
presently trickle-trickle. I rather disliked the feeling."

Two things kept this intellectual from "communing with
absolute spirit" at first. One was his own self-centered nature: "I
looked inside myself and was appalled by what I saw . . . a zoo of
lusts, a bedlam of ambitions, a nursery of fears, a harem of fondled
hatreds."

The other was a secret hope that God would not actually
interfere with his life; he wanted to retain what he considered his
freedom. But one night, to his total surprise, he experienced what
he considered a "theological shocker"; he felt a living Presence. If
it spoke, he heard it say, "I am the Lord, I am that I am." The
Presence, the Person, who had talked to him was unwelcome,
discomforting, unreasonable; he was also unrelenting. Lewis
describes this period of encountering a personal God vividly:

The real terror was that if you seriously believed in even
such a "God" or "Spirit" as I admitted, a wholly new
situation developed. . . . I was to be allowed to play at
philosophy no longer. . . . Total surrender and the absolute
leap in the dark were demanded.

You must picture me alone in that room in Magdalen,
night after night, feeling, whenever my mind lifted even for
a second from my work, the steady, unrelenting approach
of Him whom I so earnestly desired not to meet. That
which I greatly feared had at last come upon me. In the
Trinity Term of 1929 I gave in, and admitted that God
was God and knelt and prayed: perhaps, that night, the
most dejected and reluctant convert in all England.

MATTERS OF THE SOUL

I did not then see what is now the most shining and obvious thing; the Divine humility which will accept and convert even on such terms. The Prodigal Son at least walked home on his own feet. But who can duly adore that Love which will open the high gates to a prodigal who is brought in kicking, struggling, resentful, and darting his eyes in every direction for a chance of escape?

Even if Lewis's initial conversion lacked enthusiasm, he made a commitment to act on his choice and began attending his college chapel on weekdays and his parish church on Sundays—even though he disliked public worship. He also began reading St. John's gospel in Greek and began a practice he continued for the rest of his life: to read some portion of the Bible almost every day. One of the first changes his friends noticed was that Lewis exuded a new sense of happiness and enjoyment with life, relishing his afternoon walks, conversations, and books. He also started to nourish his newborn spiritual life by reading devotional literature and became especially appreciative of George MacDonald, the Scottish novelist and preacher.

The reluctant, unemotional convert then found himself infused with emotional, imaginative, vibrant stories to tell—and he gave the world a glimpse into the unique adventures of his mind. Children everywhere enjoy reading *The Lion, the Witch and the Wardrobe* in his series *The Chronicles of Narnia,* and adults have laughed at the antics of the devil in his *Screwtape Letters.* And through his many other publications and radio broadcasts he spoke honestly of his intellectual and spiritual wanderings.

What if he had chosen to say no? ◙

MATTERS
OF
THE
MIND

Introduction:
A Thinking Person's
Faith ◉

*The best treasure your Creator gave you is of course a
living intellect.*   HILDEGARD OF BINGEN

*Do not conform any longer to the pattern of this world,
but be transformed by the renewing of your mind.*
                                      ROMANS 12:2

Love the Lord your God with all your mind." Our
Creator gave us a living intellect, and we are asked to use it fully.
Notice, however, that this commandment to love God with all
your mind is not selective; no one is excluded. It's not intended
just for those with brilliant SAT scores or stunning GPAs. It's not
given to just men or just women. Each person who chooses to live
life abiding in God is asked to see his or her mind as a distinctive
gift—to be used in love. And the word *all* implies there's no
holding back.

It also implies hard work. Martin Luther King, Jr., when
trying to get people to think about America's unjust racial laws
and customs, lamented, "Rarely do we find men who willingly
engage in hard, solid thinking. There is an almost universal quest
for easy answers and half-baked solutions. Nothing pains some
people more than having to think." When we look at the
predominance of single-issue politics today, we have to wonder if
people have changed much since then.

There seems to be an unspoken fear among some students that
thinking about their religious beliefs might insult God—or that if
they dare to scrutinize their faith with their intellect, that their
faith will die, or at least diminish. They fear that if they study the

Word and the world boldly—with open, critical reflection—that somehow their sense of God won't survive.

They might be right. And that's okay—perhaps even good. Because sometimes our view of God snugly fits the title of J. B. Phillips' book *Your God Is Too Small*. We're not alone. Understanding the height and breadth of God's vision for humanity has been a common problem through the centuries. The Old Testament prophet Isaiah wrote:

> "For my thoughts are not your thoughts,
>   neither are your ways my ways," declares the Lord.
> "As the heavens are higher than the earth,
>   so are my ways higher than your ways
>   and my thoughts than your thoughts."
>   (Isaiah 55:8–9)

The longer I live, the more I see how finite my thinking is next to God's infinite justice, forgiveness, redemption, creation, compassion—the human drama we live. Each day offers a new chance of transformation, the "renewing of the mind" that God wants for us. But rather than enter the intellectual struggles of faith, we are tempted to take the easy path and divide life into compartments: my religious life, my sexual life, my intellectual pursuits, my business dealings. To search for wholeness, an integration of body, mind, and spirit, takes work—at times hard, uncomfortable work. Yet it's also invigorating and deeply satisfying.

Mental laziness, by the way, is not a problem among Christians only. The amiable agnostic or professed atheist may have the same fear of placing their beliefs in the light of intellectual inquiry. As C. S. Lewis's devil in *The Screwtape Letters* admonishes, "Don't let [people] use their minds." Obviously, if the Creator gave us an intellect, thinking can lead to loving, not denying, the Divine.

This commandment to "love the Lord with all your mind" isn't a suggestion; it's a mandate. And obviously one from a confident God, who knows that using our minds transforms the adventure of faith. For most, college will be the only time in life specifically given over to the luxury of learning. And it's not a luxury most of the world gets to enjoy. If you are among the world's privileged, it's not a time to be wasted.

Scott, now a seminary student, said he first understood this after studying in Latin America his junior year. "One week I was sick; I had amoebic dysentery, and I was out in the Honduran forest in a cabin just lying there on my cot. I started thinking about how incredibly lucky I was. Even though my parents have experienced several divorces and other things have gone wrong, I'm so wealthy because I have an education. Even if I quit now, by the world's standards I'm the cream of the crop. And I didn't deserve it by anything I did. It's just the circumstances of birth. I met Hondurans who worked so hard and didn't have a thing. I came back to America with this deep appreciation and passion to learn."

Granted, learning is risky business. Dr. Sharon Parks, former chaplain at Whitworth, in her book *The Critical Years: Young Adults and the Search for Meaning, Faith and Commitment,* tells the story of a conversation she had with a Harvard professor who had just sent his oldest son off to college. At a party the professor commented that being a parent and sending a child on to higher education felt quite different from being a professor and receiving students of other parents. Dr. Parks wrote:

> I found myself saying to him, "Well, don't worry. Whatever you are most afraid will happen to him won't. It will be something else." . . . But he quickly responded by saying, "Good. I've already decided what would be the worst thing that could happen to him." Immediately curious, I asked him what that would be. He replied, "I think the worst thing that could happen to him would be to have the time come when he would feel it was no longer possible to 'make meaning.'"

Parks, who spent years listening to students and researching how they experience faith, said, "This sensitive professor and father had named something at the very core of his son's existence; for we human beings seem unable to survive, and certainly cannot thrive, unless we can make meaning."

What scares some students about exposing their ideas to honest questions is a sense of loss, especially as they find themselves living momentarily in a land of uncertainty. During times of "in-betweenness," when our earlier ways of "making meaning" seem incomplete and we haven't conceived new ways of understanding, the landscape can look barren. No longer will black-and-white answers work, and the land of gray can get gloomy.

Almost every college asks students to reflect critically on their world, and since many institutions divide knowledge into highly specialized areas, sometimes it feels like there's more a taking apart than a pulling together of the whole. This seems especially true during the freshman and sophomore years. It can also bring a loss of innocence. Rarely can a student study American foreign policy and always say, "My country, right or wrong."

Not only does it take work to open oneself to new ideas, it takes community. Many students tell me that the late-night bull sessions, where they talk over anything and everything with their friends, teach them as much as their courses. In smaller schools, personal contacts with professors offer students time to think aloud about the ideas they are encountering. A journal is another place to think aloud, as one tries to make sense of the whole.

Besides being open to expanding our view of the world, even though it's uncomfortable, what else does this commandment mean to the college student? Unless you have come from an exceptional church community, you have probably read only smatterings of the Bible. If this is our sacred text, a guide to living life, why be ignorant of its riches?

If possible, often through course curriculums, seek out places where you can study the Scriptures in wholeness and depth, instead of staying satisfied with "hit and miss" Bible study. Universities often teach "Bible as Literature," and church-related colleges, or religion departments at other schools, usually provide classes in the Old and New Testaments. Also, find a community— even if it's only one other student—in which you can study the Bible with other thinkers. Throughout the world, whether in rural villages or innercities, Christians have helped each other by studying together, asking, "What do these words mean and how do I apply them to my life?"

This leads to the integration of the heart and mind. Martin

Luther King, Jr., stated in his sermon "Love in Action" that "one day we will learn that the heart can never be totally right if the head is totally wrong. Only through the bringing together of head and heart ... intelligence and goodness ... shall man rise to a fulfillment of his true nature."

If you follow this commandment, you will need to be patient with yourself. There is no "fast-think" restaurant for instant learning and wisdom. The Danish writer Kierkegaard, who opened his mind so fully, wrote in his journal about this need: "One does not begin feasting at dawn but at sunset. And so too in the spiritual world it is first of all necessary to work for some time before the light bursts through and the sun shines forth in all its glory."

God wants our minds to be alive, vital, questing—how else will we ever fully comprehend the magnitude of our Creator's compassion and splendor? ▣

Science
and Wonder ◙

Glory be to God for dappled things—
For skies of couple-colour as a brinded cow;
For rose-moles all in stipple upon trout that swim;
Fresh-firecoal chestnut-falls; finches' wings . . .

POET GERARD MANLEY HOPKINS

I have come to wonder if there are not about as many
sides of God as there are humans to know God, especially
now that I know more about the amazing diversity of life
forms. The great mysteries of the natural world mirror for
me the great mysteries of the Spirit. It's both humbling
and encouraging.

BIOLOGY PROFESSOR DR. LEE ANN CHANEY

When I listen to my advisees talk about taking
science courses, two distinct, polarized attitudes often emerge. One
group is eager to get started. Usually because they've experienced
fine high-school teachers, they are confident of their abilities and
look forward to the learning. But for the other group, dread and
fear dominate. They want to take "the minimum," they lack any
confidence that they could do well, and they don't even see why
colleges require it. They have decided, also often based on their
high-school experiences, that science isn't for them. Few students
seem to fall between these two poles.

What baffles me with those who avoid science is their lack of
curiosity to explore God's created universe. Seldom do they make
a connection between their faith and finding out more about the
world; if anything, they feel a subtle anxiety that engaging in
scientific inquiry might erode their faith. Yet many scientists find a
marvelous sense of awe as they study nature, an awe that shapes
the scope of their faith.

MATTERS OF THE MIND

The books of Madeleine L'Engle, contemporary author of many books, including the award-winning *Wrinkle in Time,* show a sophisticated understanding of science and the universe. In her book *Walking on Water: Reflections on Faith and Art,* she tells of a visit to a Christian college. After her presentation, a student rose and commented with some surprise, "You don't seem to feel any conflict between science and religion!"

She tried to explain:

> Of course not. Why should there be a conflict? All that the new discoveries of science can do is to enlarge our knowledge of the magnitude and glory of God's creation. We may, and often do, abuse our discoveries, use them for selfish and greedy purposes, but it is the abuse which causes the conflict, not the discoveries themselves. When they upset the religious establishment, it is not because they have done anything to diminish God; they only diminish, or even more frightening—change the current establishment's definition of God.... But our fear and our rejection does not take away from truth, and truth is what the Bible instructs us to know in order that we may be free.

Do you find yourself shutting doors to understanding our mysterious universe? If the fear of low grades keeps you from taking science classes, why not take advantage of the Pass/Fail system on many campuses? That's exactly the reason colleges instituted the policy—to encourage students to learn in areas where they are uncomfortable. You may surprise yourself and become fascinated with the vast, constantly changing fields of knowledge in environmental studies, genetics, human biology, quantum physics, chemistry, and other wonders of the universe.▣

Intellectual
Freedom ◘

I often felt stupid. European college students seem to know and care so much more about world politics than the average American. I wonder why?

A SENIOR RETURNING FROM BERLIN

And the truth will set you free.   JOHN 8:32

The free inquiry of ideas, encouraged on American campuses, is a threat in much of the world. Who can forget the Chinese students in Tienanman Square? The massacre, still denied by the Chinese government, showed what narrow intellectual limits had been imposed on the students. Persecution and arrests continue to serve notice to the Chinese people that any departures from the norms will not be tolerated.

One remnant of the squelched revolution is the televised images of courageous students longing for the freedom we take for granted in our Western world. The picture of the lone student standing in front of an oncoming tank testifies to their convictions. Or consider the Chinese students in America who persistently used FAX machines to inundate libraries in China with information about what really happened.

These same limits to free inquiry exist in other countries too. During a foreign study tour, students from seven American colleges held a secret meeting with professors and students from a major Latin American university. There they heard stories of how students in campus political groups risk death, disappearance, or imprisonment. A virtual reign of terror exists, inhibiting the student population from ever stating their ideas publicly.

One Latin American graduate student explained, "Informants can be in our classrooms. . . . It's hard to trust anyone. Because of this, it's unheard of to debate our government's policies—even in a political science, history, or government class." Consequently, class discussions avoid controversial topics or critical responses. Even the professors said they would never dare discuss their views.

The American students were astonished. "I can't imagine it," said a junior in international studies. "We spend all our class time debating policies! We're expected to be critical thinkers."

It's easy to take intellectual freedom for granted, so much so that we can become lazy thinkers. Sometimes Christians are the most reluctant to explore new ideas. Learning to see both sides of an issue and truly understand another person's point of view can create confusion, threaten our confidence, or even cause us to change our minds—all of which can be uncomfortable! Stretching our boundaries beyond our valued and preconceived notions can make us feel like we are intellectually and emotionally adrift.

Some students on our campus made this effort recently. When they arrived in September, shortly after Iraq invaded Kuwait, most of them strongly supported America's military build-up in the Middle East. Clearly, Saddam Hussein was guilty of overt aggression. He, likened to Hitler, had to be stopped. Moral right was on America's side. How could anyone support Hussein?

Then some students heard Dr. Raja Tanas, an Arab Christian from Bethlehem, present a broader history of the concerns in the region. In a one-hour lecture, this sociology professor presented an Arab perspective. Though not supporting Hussein's invasion, he longed for students to see why the Palestinians' grievances must be heard in any regional peace discussions. He raised questions about a possible American double standard that allows Israeli aggression against vulnerable Arab countries. "It's a whole other way of looking at it," remarked Sally, the daughter of a military officer. "I thought the issue was easy before today."

God promises that the truth shall set us free (John 8:32). We who are privileged to explore the wonder of the Creator's universe with open minds can learn from the courage of those who plead for this privilege in their closed societies.◙

When Choosing
a Major ▣

*It's a niche, you know, like if a bird's beak fits into a
certain place to get an insect. It's not hard for it because
it's made that way.*
A SENIOR, DESCRIBING HIS INTEREST IN SOCIOLOGY

Let me hear joy and gladness.   PSALM 51:8

Perhaps nothing frustrates the students I advise
more than their gnawing uncertainty when asked, "What's your
major?" Most colleges encourage undecided students to take a
sampling of courses that interest them for a year or two, meeting
general requirements along the way. Sometimes, often because
they can't stand living in limbo, students prematurely choose a
major and close the door to exploration.

Trying to sort out your own interests, especially if you have
many talents, is never easy. Christian writer Frederick Buechner,
while teaching at the prestigious Phillips Exeter Academy, heard
the struggles of many young men wrestling with these questions.
In his book *Wishful Thinking: A Theological ABC,* he offered one
idea for those wanting to discover the kind of work God is calling
them to: "There are all different kinds of voices calling you to all
different kinds of work, and the problem is to find out which is
the voice of God rather than of Society, say, or the Superego, or
Self-Interest."

He then encourages people to listen deeply to their own
unrecognized interests when trying to find a worthy vocation:
"The place God calls you to is the place where your deep gladness
and the world's deep hunger meet."

How do you hear your "gladness"? One way, by naming what
you really like to do. Trying new classes and experiences, so your

life decisions aren't all based on what you liked in high school. A football player, planning to major in business, told me of a great surprise he had his freshman year. Required to take a fine-arts class, he enrolled in an art course. "I absolutely loved it. It was hard to explain to my buddies what happened inside me when I was creating in the studio, but I could hardly wait to get there every day. It was unlike any joy I'd ever known." He listened to his gladness—and took more and more courses. By his senior year he had combined a business management and art degree, opening up the possibility of a lifetime of work within the arts management field. He knows what art does for the human spirit.

Do you listen to your gladness? Do you have any strong interests that also meet deep needs in our world? Are your major life decisions overly influenced by what others suggest or want for you? It will take courage to live with uncertainty, boldness to explore new areas, and a willingness to listen closely to your gladness. But in time, a sense of genuine direction should emerge. Annie Dillard, in her book *Teaching a Stone to Talk*, writes, "The thing is to stalk your calling in a certain skilled and supple way, to locate the most tender and live spot and plug into that pulse. This is yielding, not fighting." Listening to yourself to locate that tender and live spot can make all the difference.■

Our Image of God: An Obstacle? ◙

Not being tied to what God looks like, frees us.
NOVELIST ALICE WALKER

Have you thought much about your image of God or where it comes from?

One Palm Sunday morning, the pastor of a middle-class suburban church asked a young Japanese woman to say a few words. "She mentioned something in a small group recently," said the pastor from the pulpit, "and I thought it was so important, I wanted the whole congregation to hear."

So with a shaky voice, the young woman spoke. "At first, I was scared to tell you this, because I kept asking, 'What will people think of me?' But I agree it's important." Then she told her story.

"I know there is a God, but I've always sensed an obstacle that keeps me from developing a personal relationship. There's a distance . . . something separating me from a sense of closeness." Then she told a little about her church background, growing up in a Methodist church, primarily with other Japanese worshipers. Later she moved to a city with few ethnic groups and joined this primarily Caucasian congregation.

"Just recently, I realized the obstacle lies in my image of God: It's that I have mistakenly pictured God as a Caucasian male." She continued by telling how she wants to break through this barrier because she knows that's what makes her uncomfortable. Then she ended with the question: "What obstacle in your image keeps you from closeness with God?"

It's an important question, one that emerges in my conversations with students. One of the biggest obstacles for many occurs when they try to imagine God as a loving, trustworthy, faithful Father. As one student expressed it, "When your Dad's been abusive and then abandoned the family, thinking of God as a father gets in the way. How can I trust him?"

Other students harbor an image of a looming judge or resident policeman—sure to condemn their every action. Or some, fed by pictures of an ethereal wimpy Jesus, imagine a weak deity, unappealing to independent and exuberant college students.

In Alice Walker's novel *The Color Purple,* her characters speak about the images that hinder their faith. Celie, a poor, abused black woman, recounts her conversation with her friend, Shug:

> Then she say: Tell me what your God look like, Celie.
> Aw naw, I say. I'm too shame. Nobody ever ast me this before, so I'm sort of took by surprise. Besides, when I think about it, it don't seem quite right. But it all I got. I decide to stick up for him, just to see what Shug say.
> Okay, I say. He big and old and tall and graybearded and white. He wear white robes and go barefooted.
> Blue eyes? she ast.
> Sort of bluish-gray. Cool. Big though. White lashes, I say.
> She laugh.

Is the image we hold also laughable—or at the very least, limiting? Never underestimate the power of what we hold—or don't hold—in our imagination.

Why not talk with a good friend and compare your images of God? Try to figure out where they come from and which images create barriers in drawing closer to God and which ones are helpful. Or write them in a journal. ◙

Lifting Our
Blindfolds ▣

*Do not be anxious about anything, but in everything, by
prayer and petition, with thanksgiving, present your requests
to God.*   PHILLIPIANS 4:6

*One act of thanksgiving when things go wrong is worth a
thousand when things go well.*   ST. JOHN OF THE CROSS

Sometimes an unsettling event occurs that makes us
feel hostage to its negative power. For Benjamin Weir, a
Presbyterian missionary in Lebanon for thirty-one years, life
changed dramatically on May 8, 1984. While walking with his
wife to a seminary meeting, Shiite Muslims accosted him at
gunpoint on the streets of Beirut and shoved him onto the floor of
their car. From that moment, he became one more pawn in the
hostage powerplays in the Middle East.

After a terrifying car trip, his captors threw him onto a dirty
mattress in a bare room in a warehouse, chained and padlocked
him to a radiator, threatened him with a gun to his head, and then
blindfolded him. Although frightened, he was grateful to be alive.
And in his guarded room, he began to think, *What is here that
could help bring me close to a sense of the presence of God?* He
decided to risk lowering his blindfold and to let his imagination
have free reign.

Looking up he saw an electric wire hanging from the ceiling
with three wires exposed:

To me those wires seemed like three fingers ... I imagined
a hand and an arm reaching downward, like Michelangelo's
Sistine Chapel in Rome where in the fresco God is
reaching out his hand to Adam, the first created human
being. I let this remind me of God reaching toward me,

saying, "You're alive. You are mine; I've made you and called you into being for a divine purpose."

He also noticed two white circles near the ceiling—plastic covers for electrical connections. "What could they be for me, Lord. What comes in pairs?" He decided they were ears, symbolizing God hearing the cries of the saints. "So listen to me, dear God. I also surrender to your care and will."

Other sights became symbols. A stuffed bird became the peace dove; 120 horizontal slats on shutters became the "great cloud of witnesses, past and present, who through times of trial have observed the faithfulness of God." As he settled down for his first night of captivity, the song "Count Your Blessings, Name Them One by One," entered his mind. So, after counting thirty-three inch-sized links of chain between his wrist and the radiator, he started a pattern followed every night. "Thank you for life, food, a mattress, pillow, blanket, my wife, Jesus, Holy Spirit," and so on—thirty-three specific prayers of thanksgiving amidst his distress. As he finished his evening prayers, he wondered "How long, O Lord, will this go on?" He quickly slipped his blindfold back on as he heard the guard come near the door.

The "how long" became sixteen long months of captivity, mostly in total isolation, which Weir chronicles in his book *Hostage Bound, Hostage Free.* It's a contemporary faith story that powerfully shows how acts of thanksgiving in all circumstances sustained his spirit of survival.

As he consciously acted out this biblical principle, he wasn't denying his problems. "Do not be anxious about anything, but in everything, by prayer and petition, with thanksgiving, present your requests to God" (Philippians 4:6), isn't the same as Bobby McFerron's glib "Don't Worry, Be Happy" song. Instead, this means a recognition—a naming—of what is troublesome. It's a clear mandate not to practice avoidance and denial.

But after coming to God asking for Divine help, there's a twist: Come with thanksgiving. Most of us leave out this part. "I'm to be thankful that I'm failing math?" "I'm to be thankful while my parents are considering divorce?" "I'm to be thankful my engagement was just broken?"

False thanks is not what's asked for. We are not to pretend to like whatever we're worried about. I doubt Weir pretended to like being shackled to a wall. But like Weir, we can look for that one small part where we can say a genuine thanks. Perhaps it's simply: Thank you that my university provides tutors; thank you that my mom and dad both love me; thank you that you, Lord, promise to heal the brokenhearted.

What problems make you feel captive and cause you worry? Have you tried to lift your blindfold to find anything—or thirty-three things—to be thankful for in the midst? Try it and see.◙

A Commitment Move

The journey of a thousand miles begins with one step.
CHINESE PHILOSOPHER LAO-TZU

God did not give us a spirit of timidity, but a spirit of power, of love and of self-discipline. 2 TIMOTHY 1:7

Do you want a boldness of spirit and an ability to make commitments when necessary? Just as there are times when you need to pause and ponder—giving yourself room to think things through—there are other times when action proves pivotal.

Tim Hansel, an avid rock climber and director of Summit Expeditions, talks about the critical moment of commitment for climbers in his book *Holy Sweat*:

> In rock climbing there is a technical term called a "commitment move" which is often the crux move of the climb. Handholds seem scarce and footholds appear nonexistent. The tendency is to "bogart"—to freeze, to panic, to wait until exhaustion causes you, the climber, to quit the climb. You have a rope around you that will keep you from ever falling more than a few inches. But still, your first feeling is to bogart. On our Summit Expedition courses, the staff will constantly encourage the climber to "go for it." "Don't bogart! Give it your best shot!" And on a commitment move, you've either got to go for it or come off the climb.

Sometimes we desire such clear black-and-white directions for our lives, especially when a goal seems so monumental that we refuse to take even small steps forward. This passiveness fuels procrastination, limiting our lives. Yet if you read the biographies of men and women who have significantly contributed to our world, it's clear that when they took their first steps forward toward their goals, mysterious forces blessed their efforts. It happens so often that one unknown writer said:

> Until one is committed there is hesitancy, the choice to draw back, always ineffectiveness. Concerning all acts of initiative (and creation), there is one elementary truth the ignorance of which kills countless ideas and splendid plans: that the moment one definitely commits oneself, then Providence moves too.
>
> All sorts of things occur to help one that would never otherwise have occurred. A whole stream of events issues from the decision, raising in one's favor all manner of unforeseen incidents and meetings and material assistance, which no one could have dreamed would come their way.

Johann Wolfgang Von Goethe, the German playwright, once wrote, "Whatever you can do or dream you can, begin it. Boldness has genius, power and magic in it."

Is there an area in your life where timidity, lack of confidence or an unwillingness to make a commitment causes you to "bogart"—freezing you from going forward? Students tell interesting stories of their small steps toward change: mustering courage to make a phone call, which leads to a significant friendship; volunteering off campus one afternoon a week, which evolves into a career direction; taking time to fill out four scholarship applications, one of which yields a 2000 dollar award; telling a parent the truth on a sensitive subject and finding they had a similar struggle at age twenty.

A climber moves by small steps—stepping out on a ledge with faith. The call is to begin with small steps forward asking God to give the spirit of power and love and self-discipline. Where do you want to begin? ▣

A Guide for
Difficult Terrain ◉

"I'm lost."

*"Well, turn on
the light."*

*"If I knew
where the light
was, damn it,
I wouldn't be
lost."*

WRITER WENDELL BERRY

In a world where conflicting values create moral confusion, people often long for a clearer sense of "how best to live." In her book *Walking on Water: Reflections on Faith and Art,* author Madeleine L'Engle recounts a discussion she had with a student during a summer session at Wheaton College. The student asked her, "Do you think there are any absolutes?"

L'Engle thought for a moment and responded, "Yes, I think the Ten Commandments are absolutes."

Her answer didn't surprise me. In many ways, the Ten Commandments provide practical details to Christ's great command to love God and our neighbor. The first two ("Have no other gods before me" and "Do not worship graven images") speak to the ongoing issue of who or what is the center of our lives. The next two ("Do not misuse the name of the Lord" and "Keep the Sabbath day holy") show ways we demonstrate our love; the last six ("Honor your parents" and "Do not murder, commit adultery, steal, give false testimony, or covet") give a realistic account of what makes one a good neighbor.

Little has changed about human nature since God first gave Moses the Ten Commandments. If you steal your roommate's stereo, lie about the resident advisor, have an affair with your friend's wife or husband—it's not love. But the commandments also recognize the power of internal attitudes—particularly the spirit of covertness that hovers over our hearts and can prompt cheating on tests, bad-mouthing a dormmate, or taking steroids to improve athletic prowess.

What was valuable for the ancient Hebrews seems viable for the contemporary world. When I see my own teenagers leave home, my hope is that they live, by grace, following these ten clear commandments.

Why do I say, "by grace"? Because during Christ's time, a pervasive legalism surrounded these rules, coupled with a self-righteous attitude from those who thought they could achieve perfection. The overachievers judged the underachievers so that love no longer prevailed. What God gave as a loving guide was turned by humans into a judgmental whip. But the gift is still offered, and years of living bear out their wisdom.

Madeleine L'Engle, after her discussion with the Wheaton College student, went home and thought more about the Ten Commandments:

> As I set them against the great works of literature, they
> seemed to hold fast. When we break one of the
> commandments, we are doing something we would "not
> want the children to see." We are being destructive, rather
> than creative. We are taking things into our own hands
> and playing God. Playing God, hubris [pride], presumption,
> the tragic flow of all the great Greek heroes. But having
> broken the first commandment, it is almost inevitable that
> the breaking of the others will follow. Oedipus dishonors
> both his parents. Anna Karenina commits adultery. Macbeth
> is covetous. Dorian Gray makes a graven image of himself
> ... And so it goes. Whenever the first commandment is
> broken, more breakage follows. We are, as a consequence,
> unable to love ourselves, and so we are not able to love
> our neighbor.
>
> We take things into our own hands. We listen to
> promises of security, promises that can only be false. We

forget those absolutes against which we can set our behavior, make our decisions.

And we lose heart, and are no longer able to pluck out of the nettle, danger, the flower of courage.

And we draw back.

Have you ever learned the commandments? The basic version follows, and you can find the complete version in Exodus 20. Ask yourself how they apply to life today. For instance, is cheating on tests stealing? How in the world can someone keep Sundays holy while in college? In what ways could you honor your father or mother while away from home? If you creatively try to keep the commandments, you will find they provide a detailed roadmap for your journey.

———

Commandments for Loving

1. You shall have no other gods before me.

2. You shall not make for yourself an idol.

3. You shall not misuse the name of the Lord your God.

4. Remember the Sabbath day by keeping it holy.

5. Honor your father and your mother.

6. You shall not murder.

7. You shall not commit adultery.

8. You shall not steal.

9. You shall not give false testimony against your neighbor.

10. You shall not covet.◼

Discernment:
An SAT Word Worth
Remembering ◙

Dear friends, do not believe every spirit, but test the spirits to see whether they are from God, because many false prophets have gone out into the world.   1 JOHN 4:1

Have you ever encountered popular spiritual leaders or communities that seem to sow seeds of destruction and divide the people of God? It is important to be able to tell when a church or group borders on fostering a cult mentality. Discernment—the ability to understand and distinguish differences—is important.

Molly first started thinking about this issue during her senior year in high school, after attending a church youth-group meeting at which she saw a film on the Jonestown Massacre. It left her so shaken she refused to visit her home church for weeks.

Jonestown was an agricultural religious community set up in the jungles of Guyana by a persuasive American pastor, Jim Jones. He had persuaded many members of his People's Temple congregation in Ukiah, California, to leave America and set up a utopian community. These faithful followers included families with young children, college-age students, and other adults—including many concerned, service-oriented people who worked in Ukiah's Department of Social Services and Juvenile Hall.

So powerful was his hold on their minds and hearts, that he convinced nine hundred of his trusting followers to drink poisoned Kool-aid in a bizarre act of communal suicide and murder. When a few managed to slip away, they alerted authorities, who found the bloated bodies the next day.

The event stunned the church world, as it stunned Molly when she saw the film. How could devoted people of faith be so foolish? When Jones had begun his ministry in Indianapolis, it was praised as a model of interracial service to the poor. In California, he continued his focus on service to others, healing, and total commitment. But sometime during his rise to power, the emphasis on submission to Christ shifted to submission to Jim Jones.

Some discerned the danger of Jones's demand for authority. Jones's megalomania led one young man, a Wheaton College and Stanford University Law School graduate, to eventually leave Guyana. "When Jones asked, 'Why is it you won't yield yourself to me?' I knew I needed to escape." But not without cost: his only son died in the massacre.

The film made Molly ask important questions. "For the first time, it made me ask if I believe everything my church tells me. It upset me so much I couldn't bear going to church but I didn't tell anyone why." Finally, she began to talk with her youth leader and other adults, asking about things she had always taken for granted, like: "Where do the ideas I believe come from," and "How do I know they're true?"

For Molly, thinking hard about her faith led to a stronger understanding of what she believes and why. While still active in her church, she now worships out of choice, not habit.

The Jonestown tragedy was not the first, nor will it be the last, in which people blindly follow powerful leaders. The Bible warns of these false prophets. Some researchers of religious experience, such as Dr. James Fowler, believe young adults who grew up in homes without any religious thinking are most vulnerable to joining cults. He writes, "There's a religious vacuum that people feel and the invitation into an intimate community with a strong message serves as remedial religion."

How do you discern cults? When leaders subtly suggest that you follow them, not God; when they ask you to cut off your relationships with others, especially your family; when they insist their version of doctrine is the *only* truth—then it's time to be on the alert! Ask hard questions. A truly God-centered church will be delighted you asked.◙

The Class
from Hell ▣

I hate this class. I've never had a worse teacher.

A FRUSTRATED FRESHMAN

I haven't been in school for fifteen years. When I enrolled in biology, I felt the professor was speaking a foreign language.

THIRTY-FIVE-YEAR-OLD NONTRADITIONAL STUDENT

Almost inevitably most students end up in a class so difficult that they unaffectionately dub it "the class from hell." A particular course can seem impossible for lots of reasons—poor teaching, weak high-school preparation, being out of one's comfort zone, a heavy reading load, or exceptionally complex material. But for whatever reason, when one encounters such a class, the stress can color the whole term.

In most colleges and universities, students who find themselves academically drowning have several alternatives: they can change to a pass/fail grade to relieve pressure; they can drop the class if it's not required; or they can stick it out—perhaps with help from a tutor or the professor. One thing that never works is denial—the refusal to face the need for hard decisions. Most often, such students just slowly drift into failure.

Simone Weil, the brilliant French philosopher and teacher of the early 1930s, wrote about the advantages of such impossible courses. In her spiritual autobiography, *Waiting for God,* she claimed that the key to education was learning the skill of attentiveness, and she linked this skill to Christianity: "The key to a Christian conception of studies is the realization that prayer consists of attention. It is the orientation of all the attention that the soul is capable toward God." What she is saying is that difficult

MATTERS OF THE MIND

classes force us to pay attention, and that discipline can ultimately shape our receptivity to God.

Unlike many people, she is not advising students to "grit your teeth and endure"—an approach that she calls "muscular effort." Rather, she wrote, "If you say to a student, 'Now you must pay attention,' one sees them contracting their brows, holding their breath, stiffening their muscles. But the joy of learning is as indispensable in study as breathing is in running."

When a student encounters a difficult concept, Weil encourages a different kind of concentration:

> Attention consists of suspending our thought, leaving it detached, empty, and ready to be penetrated by the object; it means holding in our minds, within reach of this thought ... the diverse knowledge we have acquired. Above all, our thought should be empty, waiting, not seeking anything, but ready to receive.... We do not obtain the most precious gifts by going in search of them but by waiting for them. In every school exercise there is a special way of waiting upon truth, setting our hearts upon it.

But aren't we programmed in America to "go for it," not to "wait for it"—to become more assertive if something is difficult? Perhaps it even sounds like she is encouraging passivity and procrastination?

I don't think so. Her suggestion makes sense in light of conditions on most campuses. Finding a quiet place to study can take extra effort, and even then, while sitting alone, it is often hard to clear the mind of all the clutter of the day's activities. Just looking at a confusing textbook, math problem, or large writing project can raise one's anxiety level tremendously. "Attention," wrote Weil, "consists of suspending our thought, leaving it detached, empty, and ready." She is not talking about passivity, but an act of attention, choosing to pause and let go of the day's thoughts, allowing full receptivity to the new information ahead.

By attention, Weil means something similar to what people who pray regularly or meditate as a spiritual discipline call, "centering"—a time of emptying in order to receive. They will sometimes focus on a Bible verse to create a calm spirit, such as

"Be still and know that I am God" or "In quietness and confidence shall be my strength."

Next time you find yourself wasting energy because you are fighting against complicated material, you might want to try Simone Weil's suggestion. Everyone's learning style is different, but developing the skill of relaxed concentration often leads to a joy of learning far beyond the classroom. ◘

Journal Keeping:
A Diplomat's Diary ▣

In our era, the road to holiness necessarily passes through the world of action.
SWEDISH DIPLOMAT DAG HAMMARSKJÖLD

Complaint against God is far nearer to God than indifference about Him.
SCOTTISH WRITER GEORGE MACDONALD

Have you ever considered keeping a journal? Many college classes require them, most often English courses or off-campus learning experiences. Some professors assign them as a way of helping students develop the habit of internal and external observation and analysis. Others see it as a tool for teaching students to recognize the key experiences in their lives. Such insights can become important in choosing majors, careers, or even friends.

But journal keeping is not new; it has a rich tradition. In fact, many of the writers already mentioned in this book kept spiritual journals in which they recorded their ongoing conversations with God, their moments of praise, argument, confusion, and thanksgiving, which surround the daily events of life.

One twentieth-century diplomat, Dag Hammarskjöld, left a remarkable diary, *Markings,* which many consider a classic. A sophisticated, urban young man, he loved music, poetry, and mountain climbing. He grew up as the privileged son of a Swedish Prime Minister, and he studied law and economics at the Universities of Uppsala and Stockholm. He quickly rose to prominence in the banking and finance world and then began a distinguished career as a Swedish delegate to the United Nations. After being elected Secretary-General of the United Nations, he served from 1953 to 1961 until he died in an aircrash in Northern Rhodesia.

Over a period of many years, he wrote down his inmost thoughts, calling it "a sort of white book concerning my negotiations with myself and with God." Although he was outwardly successful, his diary reveals an inner turmoil as he spent many troubled years in a quest for meaning. He struggled with an acute awareness of his own self-centeredness, his large ego, and his desire to meet people's expectations for the son of such a prominent father.

A life-long bachelor, he wrote of his lingering loneliness and his long bouts of existential despair. Gifted in so many ways, he was not sure how to use these gifts. During his early years, he agonized over these struggles and even thought of suicide:

> What I ask for is absurd: that life shall have a meaning.
> What I strive for is impossible: that my life shall acquire a
> meaning. I dare not believe. I do not see how I shall ever
> believe that I am not alone. What makes loneliness an
> anguish is not that I have no one to share my burden, but
> this: I have only my own burden to bear.

This spirit of discouragement prevailed for many years, and then—in a subtle transformation—he found his long sought-for peace. He radically shifted his calling by aiming to forgo his own ego, forget himself, and begin living life for others. This paralleled his growing commitment to the "Way of the Cross," through which he wished to serve as an instrument of God. He described this gradual change in a 1961 entry:

> I don't know Who or What put the question, I don't
> know when it was put. I don't even remember answering,
> but at some moment, I did answer Yes to Someone—or
> something—and from that hour I was certain that existence
> is meaningful and that, therefore, my life, in self-surrender,
> had a goal. From that moment I have known what it
> means to "not look back" and "to take no thought for the
> morrow."

Hammarskjöld's inner spirit was different from that point on. No longer melancholy, he spoke of peace and wonder and joy. His

MATTERS OF THE MIND

honest account of his long, hard battle from self-centeredness to God-centeredness gives hope and patience to all of us who are trying to live a life of faith every day.

Why not begin your own journal? There are a variety of ways to approach the writing of your record of your "negotiations with God":

In a dialogue form, talk with God and imagine the response

Write down specific prayer concerns—and answers

Think aloud on paper about questions about faith. Write out your complaints against God (for instance, why is there so much suffering?)

Begin a dialogue between two sides of your personality (for instance, your trusting side and your doubting side; your generous self and stingy self)

Jot down writings or sayings that have special meaning for you

Make lists of joys for the day, pros and cons for a decision, worries, and so on

Use it alongside a Bible study

Take one area in your life you want to change (such as shyness or money management) and write about the "little steps" taken

Write out a conversation prayer

Show what happens when you are involved in service.

As a Russian proverb says: "Every day is a messenger of God." A journal gives us a concrete way to see this and a memorable record of life. Perhaps some of the following quotes from Dag Hammarskjöld's diary will get you started.

———————

For all that has been, Thanks
For all that will be, Yes

Never measure the height of a mountain until you have reached the top. Then you will see how low it is.

So shall the world be created each morning anew,
forgiven, in Thee, by Thee.

Don't be afraid of yourself, live your individuality to
the full but for the good of others.

Hallowed be Thy Name
    not mine,
Thy Kingdom come,
    not mine
Thy Will be done,
    not mine

Give us peace with Thee
    Peace with men
    Peace with ourselves
And free us from all fear.◙

Breaking the Barriers of Imagination ◙

And by my God I can leap over a wall.
2 SAMUEL 22:30, NEW AMERICAN STANDARD BIBLE

Blessed are the peacemakers, for they will be called sons of God.
MATTHEW 5:9

When two visiting Germans sat in front of our television to watch the celebration after the collapse of the Berlin Wall, they were mesmerized. Attacking the wall with a sledge-hammer? Gathering chunks as souvenirs? Dancing and singing on the ledge while armed East German guards just smiled?

"It's unbelievable," said Annerose Grusser, a high-school teacher from West Germany.

"It's unthinkable," added Andreas Peretz, a twenty-eight-year-old graduate student at the Technical University in Berlin. Stunned, they tried to absorb this swiftly tilting history of their homeland.

My husband and I, who have led January-term trips to Berlin, watched with equal astonishment. Our college originally offered this winter-abroad program because we were convinced that this divided city provided a unique window on the complex world of East-West relationships. It was a laboratory for many of the concerns of the Western world: the impact of two world wars, co-existence amid ideological differences, and the relationship be-tween church and state. Students also find in cosmopolitan Berlin a city bursting with creative expression in the form of magnificent museums, orchestras, and theaters.

Our trip always included a visit to East Berlin, often an anxiety-producing experience for young Americans raised on the emotional and intellectual remnants of the Cold War. Nothing pierces their walls of fear more than meeting East Germans, talking with church leaders in a communist world, seeing moms and dads sledding with children, or enjoying chance conversations with university students.

Even the guards seem more human. As one student said, "I remember my surprise when I saw a young soldier guarding the wall by the Reichstag. He looked so much like my little brother. I wondered if he liked to play soccer and go to dances?"

While we valued those breakthroughs in their walls of understanding, we could offer no hope at that time that the actual physical walls in Berlin would ever come down. Most Berliners hated the repression it symbolized, but they lived with it in grudging acceptance.

Then a few East Germans, committed to change, made the world realize that we had all suffered from a "poverty of imagination" concerning the prospect of their freedom. The pressure they exerted, fueled by the frustrations of millions, rocked a repressive political establishment and unleashed a movement faster than anyone could have imagined. And at its core were leaders in the East German church.

As Jim and I raised our glasses in a toast to Andreas and Annerose, rejoicing for their country, I couldn't help but feel a certain sadness for our own. Have we built impenetrable walls around our own country, holding our planet in nuclear bondage? If the Berlin Wall is the visible symbol of the Cold War, isn't the invisible wall that encircles our globe more insidious? One barrier is built of concrete and barbed wire; the other with East-West distrust and fear—what we think and believe about each other. One restricts travel rights and political expression; the other waits poised with power to destroy life.

Never doubt that we are captives in our own way. Our homeless, our decaying inner cities, our infant death rates, our neglected environment, and our drug and alcohol problems—all cry out for money that is presently given to military spending. Who can measure the cost to the human spirit, especially for our young people, when the hope for substantial change in the political landscape is considered naïve and impractical.

The madness is mutual, as Mikhail Gorbachev well knows. The Soviet Union, with its soaring defense costs, also desperately needs to free funds for nagging domestic issues.

When a few bold dreamers, the minority voices, challenge us to consider a "nuclear free world," the unspoken response is "it's unthinkable." Partial disarmament maybe—but beware of bold strokes. And while we have a vague belief that "no one will push the buttons," do we realize that a belief can put a stop to it? Or because of our individual helplessness, do we adopt an attitude of resignation and unconsciously choose to leave a hostage-bound planet to our children?

But why? What creates this mindset? "It seems so stupid, Mom," expressed our seventeen-year-old daughter, Krista, when thinking about our nuclear-dominated world. "Deep down, we all know nuclear weapons are wrong. We don't want another bomber; we want peace. Can't we get past our fears?" I'm sure her voice echoes the hearts of every American and Russian adult and child.

We're at a wonderful historic moment. Because of the immense power of telecommunication, the whole world has watched Berlin with fascination. Together, East and West, we have seen with our own eyes a seemingly immovable symbol of outdated thinking tumble down. We have also seen the power of a small community of committed citizens to shape their destiny.

Why can't the same insistent forces for freedom tapped for one nation be tapped for an entire planet? Why not build on the energy of this grand celebration for Germans and imagine a magnificent world celebration the day our invisible wall comes down? We need to face without flinching the truth of the terror we have created. And "peace-by-peace," we need to work together to dismantle this hidden wall.

The timing couldn't be better. Unprecedented efforts are underway for significant disarmament negotiations; our leaders need to hear of our bold support.

The words of one of our early American founders could help restore our clouded vision. In 1630, shortly before landing in New

England, John Winthrop, first governor of Massachusetts, spoke on the ship *Arabella* to the small band of Puritans. Knowing the dangers inherent in creating a new nation, he said, "The only way to avoid shipwreck and to provide for our posterity is to follow the counsel of Micah—to do justly, to love mercy, and to walk humbly with our God. For this end we must be knit together in this work as one; we must entertain each other in brotherly affection; we must be willing to abridge ourselves of our superfluities for the supply of others' necessities."

Can't we agree that nuclear weapons are superfluous? Can't we insist on using our resources and energy to supply others' necessities? Imagine the Puritans returning to the nation they founded with such hope, faith, and sacrifice? "What?" they might say. "They've built bombs that could destroy this beautiful world? They're still building them? And they don't care?"

Wouldn't they say, "It's unthinkable. It's unbelievable." Can't we agree? ▣

MATTERS
O F
STRENGTH

Introduction:
Strength for
the Journey ▣

Mono and macho don't mix.
A RUGBY PLAYER WITH MONONUCLEOSIS

If you falter in times of trouble, how small is your strength!
PROVERBS 24:10

Loving the Lord with all your strength links physical with mental strength. It is a call to active, intentional love merging body and mind in a way that physiologists understand well. The body matters. And any college student knows that when the body is run down, exhausted, or sick, it affects all their mental efforts. Adademics suffer; friendships suffer; work suffers.

The opposite is also true. We watch in awe when we see finely disciplined, motivated athletes perform feats of excellence and grace. Their beautiful strong bodies and obvious concentration remind us of the extraordinary possibilities within those who choose to test their strength.

I have often thought if Jesus chose to visit a campus and befriend college students, he would probably advise them, "Don't forget to take care of yourself." To stay physically strong takes diligence—you have to take charge of your life.

It's similar to riding a kayak through white-water rapids. Milt Prigee, a newspaper cartoonist, described to me his experiences learning to kayak and the parallels he saw in the spiritual life. A kayak has no rudder, which leaves it free to spin and wander at every whim of the current. Unless they want the river deciding their direction, the rowers must take charge and depend on the strength of their arms to negotiate the rapids.

Prigee began training in a swimming pool, practicing "eskimo rolls" (getting right side up again after flipping upside down), and paddling techniques, all of which prepared him for the dangerous rapids that give such a sense of adventure to the sport.

"Our coach kept explaining, 'Once you enter the river, you must take charge and move the paddle faster than the water moves. You'll get scared, but you've got to gut it out. Either you steer or the water steers you and throws you wherever it wants. That's the danger. You've got to negotiate the rocks, make quick decisions, and stay ahead. Whatever happens don't let go of your paddle.'"

Prigee thought he understood this—until his maiden voyage. "The river hurls you so fast, you've got to barrel through your terror. I didn't get ahead of the river, and sure enough—it started tossing me around. I hit the rocks; they whipped me around; I lost the paddle and flipped into the icy water. Fortunately, my coach was there to rescue me."

Staying healthy on a college campus takes as much intelligent negotiation as kayaking in a white-water river. Everything is disrupted: sleeping in noisy dorms; eating at irregular times; working long, strange hours to finance an education. With the new freedom of being able to determine your own hours, habits, social life, it is easy to miscalculate the minimum requirements for essential health. And like a sudden rock in a turn in the river, a bout of flu can sabotage a student's schedule; or an athletic injury can sap energy and require hours of hospitalization and therapy; or an emotional upset can destroy concentration on academics. And no mom or coach can rescue you. "I never planned on being sick so much," reflected a varsity volleyball player in describing a troublesome frosh year.

Rarely do juniors and seniors operate with the same abandonment and personal omnipotence that characterize the first few months of college. They have learned their limits through trial and error, and know how to maintain reservoirs of strength for the demands of midterms and finals. Wisdom emerges. Like the kayaker, they do not want to be tossed to and fro. Those who don't, often become college statistics—part of the 40 percent who drop out.

For survival, once you enter college you need to take charge and take care. Abuse of the body—whether with alcohol or drugs, sleep deprivation, or eating habits—sabotages strength. It's like going down the rapids surrounded by boulders—without a paddle. Without control, you will be spun around and eventually flipped. Listen to your body—know what it needs.

Mental strength also demands endurance and perseverence— and it's not easily breakable or fragile. Greg LeMond won the Tour de France after his shotgun injury by staying mentally positive—and learning patience with a healing body. The Detroit Pistons are renowned for their mental toughness under pressure. Heather, by age eighteen, had battled three bouts of cancer since she was six; she is now entering college because of her indomitable spirit. All of these people refused to give in.

It also takes mental strength to "barrel through your terror." You may be one of the lucky students who thrive immediately in college. But for many, depression occurs off and on. Many float for months in discouragement—triggered by homesickness for friends and family, their inadequate study habits and the resulting low grades, a loss of identity—or whatever.

For some, leaving home may allow painful memories to surface in a stark way. Anger and a sense of betrayal may erupt as they face the aftereffects of sexual abuse, alcoholism, neglect, or the break-up of the family. Many write research papers as a way of understanding what happened to them. Dealing with these issues during early adulthood is so important that almost every college offers free resources—which is not always the case for adults outside of the college environment. Support groups for adult children of alcoholics, bulimics, anorexics, and children of divorce exist on many campuses. And most colleges offer private counseling.

Those students who barrel through their terror often emerge with a mental exhilaration and inner peace. They can eskimo roll when they flip and often turn their pain into a tool for learning, sometimes even entering careers to help others cope with similar experiences.

And God promises us rich resources. When we come to the end of our ability, we're encouraged to ask for help. "His power is made perfect in weakness" (2 Corinthians 12:9). "Be strong and courageous," says the Lord, "and I myself will be with you" (Deuteronomy 31:23). ◘

Lesson from a Champ: Patience in Plateaus ▣

Those who hope in the Lord
will renew their strength.
They will soar on wings like eagles;
they will run and not grow weary,
they will walk and not be faint.

ISAIAH 40:31

In this world you will have trouble. But take heart! I
have overcome the world.

JOHN 16:33

Sometimes a great athlete comes along and captures the heart of a fickle public. In the summer of 1989, during the famous Tour de France bicycle race, the world watched with fascination as champion cyclist Greg LeMond battled to overcome enormous odds. He had been the first American to win the grueling twenty-three day, 2000-mile tour in 1986, but he found that his fortunes changed abruptly in 1987 when an accident nearly cost him his life. While on a hunting trip, he was accidentally shot in the back with buckshot. Four months into his slow recuperation, Greg faced an emergency appendectomy. After that, when he was finally able to begin training again, he developed an inflamed shin and had to quit. Trials, tribulation, distress, and frustration.

In an article in *Sports Illustrated,* LeMond talked of his efforts to return to his beloved sport: "The last two years have been the most humiliating of my life. Riders and team managers thought I was damaged goods." When he fared poorly in his initial races, the Dutch team wanted to cut his salary significantly. "They lost total confidence in me. They were trying to claim that maybe my liver was bad, my lung was shot up, maybe I had lead poisoning. That's why I wasn't riding well. Basically they said, 'Maybe you're not going to ever come back.'"

For LeMond, who always knew he wanted to return to cycling, the hard part wasn't the demanding training, but being patient until his body was ready. His body recovered slowly by going through a series of plateaus, and each plateau required a period of adaptation. To reach each new plateau, LeMond had to stretch his endurance. Then he had to allow his body time to recuperate before stretching it again to reach a higher level. Waiting out the plateaus continually tested his patience. "No matter how dedicated you are, how seriously you train, you need a certain period of time to do that. It's impossible to go straight there."

In the Tour of Italy, he did so poorly that the doctors tested his blood and found he was anemic. "I was pushing so hard I was eating into my muscle." Doctors gave him injections of iron to give new strength. In May, shortly before the Tour de France, he entered another race, the Tour de Trump, hoping to do well. Instead, he couldn't stay with anyone on the hills and finished twenty-seventh. He almost quit.

Instead, he set modest goals for the Tour de France, hoping perhaps to be in the top twenty and maybe to win one of the twenty-one stages that would allow him the joy of wearing the yellow jersey. His name was never mentioned by the press in the pre-race favorites. Most cyclists followed Pedro Delgado of Spain, the 1988 winner, or else they paced themselves against the two-time winner, Frenchman Laurence Fignon.

During the first twenty-two days of the race, Greg's physical and mental strength surprised everyone, including himself. LeMond fought tenaciously. He deceded the steep alpine peaks of the Pyranees at a dangerous sixty miles per hour and raced against the clock, the wind, and the other racers. By the final day, LeMond looked like he had a good chance of coming in in the top three. Fignon led by 50 seconds going into the short, 15.2 miles final time trial into Paris. No one thought Greg could smash through that insurmountable barrier—except Greg himself.

MATTERS OF STRENGTH

"It's still possible," he said to himself. "I know I can win." Then, he put his head down and rode as fast and smart as he could, with total concentration—even refusing to have his concentration interrupted with information on his times. When he neared the finish line at the Arc de Triomphe at 26 minutes and 57 seconds, he was the fastest of the day by an astounding 33 seconds. When Fignon arrived, his 58-second distance gave LeMond a mere 8-second victory after 87 hours of racing!

On the victory platform, LeMond thought back to the events of the past two years with a sort of wonder. "I kept thinking about how I almost quit two months ago, and what a good thing it was that I never gave up early. That's what it taught me. Never give up early." In 1990 he won again, placing himself as one of history's enduring cycling champions.

Patience during plateaus, self-discipline to reach goals, believing in yourself even when others don't, persistence in spite of pain—these are the marks of a true champion. All this to ride a bike and gain the world's fame. Doesn't the God of the Universe deserve followers with similar grit? ◙

Celebrations
Great and Small ▣

The Lord reigns, let the earth be glad.   PSALM 97:1

The week before Thanksgiving break, Dexter was depressed. All his dormmates were counting the days before they could take off for home, but Dexter wouldn't be leaving. He was a basketball player at a major university, and the entire team had to stay on campus to practice. "I was really bummed," he told me later. "I missed home like never before."

Then a care package came in the mail. "My mom sent Thanksgiving to me: scented candles, makings for a pumpkin pie, turkey napkins, homemade decorations for my room, candy corn—everything that makes me think of home. Mom's thoughtfulness totally turned my spirits around." Missing his home also deepened his sense of what being in a family means. Dexter's mom had nudged him into creating his own celebration.

I once heard a Christian family psychiatrist (who was in the process of getting a divorce) say, "The problem in Christian homes is we don't celebrate enough." He may have understood something about the strength people in almost every culture receive from taking the time out to celebrate life.

Writer Byrd Baylor has recently written a book called *I'm in Charge of Celebrations*. Although she wrote it for children, it is like *The Velveteen Rabbit* in that it can be read and loved by adults as well. Its heroine lives alone in the desert among the beargrass, yuccas, cacti, rocks, coyote trails, and hawk nests. People often ask her, "Aren't you lonely out there with just the desert around you?"

"How could I be lonely?" she responds. "I'm the one in charge of celebrations. Last year I gave myself 108, besides the ones they close school for." Then the book shows, with exquisite artwork by

Peter Parnall, what she celebrated: a triple rainbow in a canyon, a swirl of dustdevils, a sky of falling stars and green clouds.

Celebration means looking at the commonplace from a new angle. Anticipating planned celebrations—a birthday party, Christmas festivities, a summer picnic—gives us the feeling of "I can't wait . . ." But unexpected celebrations can brighten a dull day as well. In our college town, students often drive forty-five minutes up the winding roads to Mount Spokane, just to find a clearing and spread a picnic feast. In winter a plastic sled gives hours of pleasure. Or in summer they go ice-blocking, when store-bought blocks of ice become sleds on the grass.

Tired of sweats and jeans, some students at an East-Coast college dressed up in semi-formals for dinner one night. On Halloween one dorm group decorated their halls and invited children from the nearby public housing project for trick or treats. "We probably had more fun than the kids," recalls a junior.

Celebration is a way to say thank you for the miracles of everyday life. Dom Helder Camara, like the author of *I'm in Charge of Celebrations,* believes each day—every moment even—rings with reasons to sing a song to the Creator. In his poem "A Thousand Reasons for Living" he writes:

> If you have a thousand reasons for living,
> if you never feel alone,
> if you wake up wanting to sing,
> if everything speaks to you,
> from the stone in the road
> to the star in the sky,
> from the loitering lizard
> to the fish, lord of the sea,
> if you understand the winds
> and listen to the silence,
> rejoice,
> for love walks with you
> he is your comrade,
> he is your brother.

Is there something you want to celebrate today? ▣

When You Feel Inadequate ▣

A man's got to know his limits.
GREAT AMERICAN THEOLOGIAN (AND ACTOR)
CLINT EASTWOOD

*My grace is sufficient for you, for my power is made
perfect in weakness.*   2 CORINTHIANS 12:9

Do you sometimes—maybe often—feel inade-
quate? It's inevitable in a competitive college atmosphere. If a
student takes challenging courses, participates in athletics, or
performs in the arts, he or she will often face times of genuine
inadequacy. But some people have a way of turning their
inadequacies into assets, while others only bemoan their fate.

Actually, a rich sense of inadequacy can act as a springboard to
a deeper determination. At the very least, it keeps us humble! One
young man, hampered by a severe stutter, imaginatively overcame
his limitation. When he wanted to ask a certain young woman to a
dance, he called her three times. Each time his nervousness kept
him from being able to get the words out. In frustration, he
designed a colorful poster that asked in bold letters: "Kim, will
you go to the dance with me? Chris."

At 2:00 A.M. he secretly placed it in front of her dorm. When
she discovered it the next morning, she—and all of her dorm
friends—were touched and amused by his inventiveness. She
quickly told him yes! Chris took his problem and let it lead him
into a distinctive solution.

Academic inadequacy is seldom as easy to overcome. But
many times classroom difficulties stem from poor preparation, not
from a lack of intelligence, which means the problem is solvable—
with work. Jan remembers this well. While living in a series of

foster homes during her rebellious high-school years, she never studied—and she barely graduated. Fifteen years later, when a friend asked her, "Do you want to be a waitress all your life?" she decided, at thirty-three, to try college. Admitted on probation, she studied constantly and surprised herself with the quality of her academic work. During her first semester, she earned a 3.0.

But during a January-term course, when she tackled her first science class in biology, her sense of inadequacy almost paralyzed her. "It was a three-week intensive course," she recalls, "with three exams, five reports, a book review, and final paper. I was having to learn a whole new language and to think scientifically in a foreign terminology. I began to panic."

Scared, she sought help from a college counselor. "I saw I was painting myself into a corner," Jan explained to me. "I was telling myself 'I don't understand' and then refusing to listen. I wasn't problem solving."

The counselor showed her all the options the college offered: tutors, librarians, professors, test-taking workshops. "But it was up to me to reach out and ask," said Jan. "The counselor showed me it's okay not to know something, but I had to seek assistance myself." Jan's nerve returned, and she eventually not only conquered her science course, but graduated with honors.

St. Paul's story is similar. In 2 Corinthians 12:7–10, he tells of his "thorn in the flesh"—a mystery that no one can identify for sure. But we do know that three times he asked the Lord to have it leave him. God's answer? A resounding no—after which Paul changed both his attitude and his prayer. No longer did he ask to lose his infirmity, because he believed God had answered, "My grace is sufficient for you, for my power is made perfect in weakness." Instead, Paul saw it as a gift. "Therefore I will boast all the more gladly about my weaknesses, so that Christ's power may rest on me. . . . For when I am weak, then I am strong."

In what areas of your life do you feel inadequate? Is there a way for these inadequacies to force you to draw on your inner strength or creativity? Or do they demand a deeper, humbler reliance on God's power? If you have never felt inadequate, could it be that you are choosing challenges that are much too small? ◘

Break-Time:
In Praise of
Public Places ▣

*I think it pisses God off if you walk by the color purple
in a field somewhere and don't notice it.*
        NOVELIST ALICE WALKER IN *THE COLOR PURPLE*

Someone once asked Albert Einstein what he
thought was the most important question we could ask about life.
His answer? "The most important question is, 'Is the universe a
friendly place or not?'"

One thing spiritual leaders of almost every religious tradition
have in common is a love for the natural world; they find their
souls restored when they pause to enjoy God's friendly earth.
William Apel, the chaplain at Linfield College in Oregon, writes
of this in his book *Witnesses Before Dawn* as he describes the life of
American preacher Howard Thurman. Co-founder of the first
truly integrated church in the United States, the Church of the
Fellowship of All Peoples, in San Francisco in 1944, Thurman was
also the first black to hold a full-time faculty appointment at
Boston University. *Life* magazine recognized him as one of the
twelve greatest preachers of modern America. As a child, amid the
bitter racism of the South, he found solace through nature—the
woods near his home, the ocean, and a single magnificent oak in
his backyard:

> I needed the strength of that tree, and like it, I wanted to
> hold my ground. . . . I could reach down in the quiet
> places of my spirit, take out my bruises and my joys,
> unfold them and talk about them.

The tree became Thurman's most trusted boyhood friend:

There were times when it seemed as if the earth and the river and sky and I were one beat of the same pulse. . . . There would come a moment when beyond the single pulse beat there was a sense of Presence which seemed to speak to me. There was no voice. There was no image. There was no vision. There was God.

Native Americans share a rich tradition of reverence for the earth. The Hopi, one of the Pueblo Indian tribes, live in what some would consider the most desolate part of southwest Arizona. Yet known as the "people of peace," they affirm the friendliness of the earth in all their acts, living to sing the song of the Creator.

The Psalmist also understood this. In the famous Psalm 23, David, the future Jewish king of Israel, sings:

> *The Lord is my shepherd,*
> *I shall not want.*
> *He makes me lie down in green pastures,*
> *he leads me beside quiet waters,*
> *he restores my soul.*

We don't need to own land to experience the beauty of creation. In almost every community, there are parks, trails, and waterways that have been set aside for the public. About twenty minutes from our campus is one public area called Indian Painted Rock, because there are original hieroglyphics where Native Americans wrote on large granite bolders. The county built a trail to encourage visitors. Beyond the rocks, the trail winds down through meadows surrounded by ancient hillsides of pine trees, Oregon grape, and mock orange blossoms; then it follows the Little Spokane River, a gentle paradise for canoe enthusiasts. In spring, the river meanders through acres of golden iris under the cottonwood trees. It's a breathtaking sight—reminiscent of a Monet painting. College students often visit on Saturdays or Sundays.

One year, on the first day of spring, my husband and I hiked these trails after the snowmelt and looked for yellow buttercups. As we rounded a bend in the river, we found a sun-warmed rock and sat beside the still waters. While pausing, we saw a log on which five large turtles were lazily sunning themselves. I don't know if turtles smile, but these water creatures looked as grateful as teenagers greeting the first rays of tanning sunshine.

On a much grander scale, Stanley Park in Vancouver, British Columbia, is one of the most exquisite parks in any bursting metropolis. Its founder's dream was to bring the beauty of the country into the city. Near the start of the trail that winds around the thousand-acre park is a welcome sign that reads: "For all nations, creeds and races."

On one early summer day when our family visited, it seemed like a little United Nations. Along the shores of the Pacific Ocean harbor, a Japanese toddler built a sand castle, a young African man rode a bike, an East Indian couple strolled on the promenade exclaiming over the rhododendrons and azaleas in bloom. Nearby a Chinese grandfather rested on a park bench enjoying the waddle of Canadian geese; a Sikh in a wheelchair relished the sun; and a Nisqua Indian tribe apprentice carved a totem pole, while fascinated visitors watched his skill at this vanishing craft.

Are there public places near your college where you can slip away for a few hours to refresh your spirit and restore your soul? Does your campus provide points of beauty—gardens, reflecting ponds, grassy picnic areas? God offers every person gifts from the earth. We can choose to walk past them or to pause and take time to enjoy the extravagance of the everyday, simple things of creation.◙

Stressing Out— or Working Out ◙

He gives strength to the weary and increases the power of the weak.   ISAIAH 40:29

Just Do It.   NIKE AD

On almost every campus, around 3:30 in the afternoon, a metamorphosis takes place. Students shed their backpacks and books, and change into clothes that give them freedom to run, swim, row, kick soccer balls or footballs, play tennis or volleyball or frisbee golf—or whatever else gives them enjoyment and helps relieve stress. Most students realize that physical exertion invigorates their spirits and bodies to face a night of more study. Most, but not all.

Steve, a leading high-school athlete in basketball and tennis, didn't see the need for this "time-waster" in college. As a nearly straight-A student in high school, he was scared about grades in college. "I'd heard it's common to drop a full grade point in college, so I decided not to play any sports my first year. Actually, I'd rarely studied in high school, and I was afraid my sloppy study habits might catch up with me."

So Steve studied and studied and studied. Carrying a heavy academic load fall term, including physics and calculus, he diligently used every spare moment to crack the books. If he had an hour between classes, he wouldn't think of joining a quick game at the Hub pool table or jogging with his roommate.

"After taking my first physics test," he said, "I felt confident and told everyone I had probably gotten an A. When I received a C minus, I was absolutely shocked."

This reinforced his earlier theory about the drop in college grades, so he responded by studying even more—this time after midnight. "For the first time in my life," says Steve, who sees himself as normally light-hearted and fun-loving, "I started getting really moody. Someone would knock on my door and I wouldn't answer. Or if my roommate didn't pick up his clothes, I'd blow up."

He also became jealous of the varsity basketball players and struggled with losing his identity as an athlete. "After all my high-school achievements, I was used to having strangers come up after games and say, 'Good job.' Now I felt like a nobody."

By the middle of the term, Steve's resident advisor noticed the changes and suggested to Steve that he might actually be studying too much. "It was the best thing that happened to me," said Steve. "The advisor said, 'You might be wiser to accept a bad grade every now and then than to be in a continual state of stress.'"

One night, feeling especially tense, Steve pushed his calculus book away, grabbed his basketball, and ran over to the intramural gym. "I just shot balls for two hours by myself. I couldn't believe how different I felt after that. I now realize I'm the kind of guy who needs the release and relaxation of sports; it'd been such a part of my life growing up. So I started making a habit of shooting and joining pick-up games."

After recognizing the importance of physical activity, Steve approached his original academic goals with a more refreshed spirit. He was able to relax with his friends and to maintain exceptional grades, enough to earn a coveted graduate fellowship. Once he established a healthy balance of physical and mental activity in his life, he even joined the tennis team. "I saw that the Lord gave me my strength and my love of sports. To deny this was stupid."

But you don't need to be a dedicated athlete to benefit from exercise. A professor of psychology, Dr. Robert E. Thayer, tried an experiment at California State University in Long Beach. Taking students on a moderately fast ten-minute walk increased their sense of energy, improved moods, and even helped reduce test anxiety. "A far better pick-up than eating a candy bar," he explains in his *Psychology Today* article on "Energy Walks."

Other research has shown the importance of exercise to both physical and mental health. It seems our twentieth-century sedentary lifestyle breaks the balance of God's original design for the human body. Colleges recognize this and offer all levels and kinds of physical activity—from individual participation to physical education classes, from intramural to varsity sports. Could this help you de-stress? ◨

Eating Disorders that Disable ◨

I have to drop out this semester; I've been hospitalized again for bulemia.   A TWENTY-YEAR-OLD SOPHOMORE

People think it's just a young woman's disease, but I've been fighting this in secret for seven years.
A THIRTY-FIVE-YEAR-OLD MOTHER RETURNING TO
COLLEGE

Perhaps the saddest hallmark of America's obsession with thinness is the high number of cases of anorexia-nervosa and bulemia. Each term, intelligent, attractive, confused women (and even some men) enter classes with a history of one or both of these eating disorders. "We've got a bulemia epidemic in our dorms," stated one senior from an East-Coast church-related college.

With all the new stresses that college brings, a sense of powerlessness can prevail the first year—and can cause many freshmen to revert to earlier destructive patterns. It can sometimes hook new converts into the vicious cycle.

One second-semester freshman from the Midwest attended a university of 9,000 in the East. Fifteen hundred miles from home, living in a graduate dorm, she was miserable first semester and ate for comfort. By second semester she panicked. "I became so obsessed with my weight that I'd go running at night, sometimes for hours. No one knew I had a problem, because running allowed me to binge privately. Everyone said, 'Oh, you look great; you're really in shape,' when I lost almost thirty pounds in a month."

She was a bright student but had an uneven academic record. So when academic pressure intensified, so did her habits. "I had this brilliant woman professor from Stanford that I really respected. When I had to write papers for her, I panicked. I would get nauseated, and the problem went straight to my stomach. I would overeat, throw up, and then eat for hours and hours. Or I would go through swings where I'd gain weight for a month and then try fasting and purging and frantic exercise for a month."

Shortly before the end of the term, her health problems and depression grew so severely that she dropped out, losing the entire semester's credit. It's a common story.

At the same time, I meet other women who battle eating disorders with courage and win. These overcomers have some traits in common. First, they are honest about their problem with themselves and with others. Second, they ask for family and roommate support. Some try to understand the illness by using assigned research papers to study the causes and cures. And if they slip back into patterns, they don't hide it; they seek professional help immediately.

If you want to love the Lord with all your strength but find yourself stuggling with an eating disorder, seek all the resources available to conquer this potentially deadly disease. If a friend battles with it, let her or him know there's help available, usually right on campus.

The biggest dangers are denial and trying to keep it a secret. The sooner you face the truth and ask for help, the greater the chance to break a destructive pattern. There's lots of support available—but only if you ask.◙

LOVING YOUR NEIGHBOR

Introduction:
Beyond Ourselves ◘

Community is the place where God completes our lives with his joy.
> CONTEMPORARY WRITER HENRI J. M. NOUWEN

Whatever God does, the first outburst is always compassion.
> MEDIEVAL MYSTIC MEISTER ECKHART

All of God's people should have at least a simple decent place to live.
> MILLARD FULLER, FOUNDER OF HABITAT FOR
> HUMANITY

What does it mean to love your neighbor on a college campus? Do you have to stop studying for a physics exam because your roommate argued with her boyfriend and needs to talk? Do you devote all of your free time to service projects in the community? It is tempting to think that acts of caring involve responding to immediate and obvious needs. But there's another way to look at it.

When my husband and I were newlyweds, he used to talk about love "for the long haul." I hated the phrase then—it seemed so unromantic. It also seemed like an excuse not to give each other attention on the "short haul," those day-by-day signs of love that make marriage so enjoyable. But to him it symbolized the strength he had seen in his parents' enduring marriage, as he watched their faithful spirits survive the raising of three sons, financial pressures, business disappointments, and illness.

College seems to be a place where understanding the difference between loving your neighbor in the "long haul" and the "short haul" makes a lot of sense.

At a recent college graduation, the commencement speaker said, "If you want, you can waste a perfectly good life by chasing money." I assume you plan and need to earn money, but you probably want something more—and you probably don't want to waste your life. If you see college as a way of learning skills to provide for yourself and family, plus preparing you in some way to serve and influence the world for good, then the day-by-day dedication you direct toward studies is an act of love to your future neighbor. That's looking at love in the long haul.

For instance, if you're preparing in a specific field—like music education, sports medicine, law, engineering, architecture, aerospace mechanics, culinary arts—with a goal in mind, the more you learn now equips you to serve your neighbor better in the future. Dr. Dale Brunner, a New Testament scholar and professor, spoke once to college students at Hollywood Presbyterian Church and alluded to this "long haul" love. At the time, many students were feeling pressured by some para-church organizations to give considerable time to a "beach evangelism" program of outreach to the unchurched. The students felt torn. They knew this had importance in God's commission, but they had trouble keeping up with academics at UCLA and USC. He offered an alternative vision.

"If I'm having open-heart surgery," he said, "I'm very hopeful that my surgeon gave his very best while in med school and didn't spend valuable study time evangelizing on the beach. I don't want a surgeon cutting me up that slipped by on the minimum. Cracking the books shows love." He wasn't advocating that students miss out on significant ways of volunteering in their community and church; he was simply giving them permission to think of studies as an act of love.

While in graduate school, I met a young scientist from Holland who was working on a Ph.D. During college, he had been a leader in student protests in Europe. These public demonstrations included environmental issues in his country—a land abundant with waterways. Then he took a long look at the problems and his talents. He decided the best way to help his country's problems and be part of the solution was to learn all he could about cleaning up the environment. It took years in

LOVING YOUR NEIGHBOR

American universities, investigating such unromantic topics as using sludge for organic farming, monitoring Washington-State rivers for purity, devoting hundreds of hours in the lab. But eventually he returned to serve his country and is now one of the nation's top specialists and a teacher who passes on his knowledge to the next generation. He lived out his love in the long haul by studying water resources and management.

But what if you haven't decided on a major? Or what if you plan to graduate with a general humanities degree? Even then, much of your coursework will specifically prepare you to understand others. History, sociology, psychology, literature, political science—all build a foundation for insight into people, structures of culture, and issues of justice. Many colleges offer excellent cross-cultural courses, either abroad or on campus, which can place you on fast-forward in understanding another's world.

Whatever you choose to study, if you pursue it with intellectual discipline and commitment, it will be an act of loving your future neighbor. It feels intangible now. It may not have immediate gratification. But never underestimate its worth.

Then there's the short haul. A college is a mini-laboratory in which to learn to understand our world. That's why the current flare-ups of bigotry on some campuses are so unsettling—"If college students can't learn to get along, who will?" lamented one journalist.

Tensions emerge because college brings together people who haven't known one another before. Living together in one university dorm may be eighteen- to twenty-two-year-olds from vastly different geographic and cultural backgrounds. Part of love in the short haul is simply getting to know people who are different from us. "I slowly see myself coming out of the protective shell I'd put around myself during high school," stated one freshman, who valued getting past her limiting teenage friend-ships.

Learning to love your neighbor when you don't particularly like him or her presents another challenge. Inevitably, there will be roommates, professors, teammates, work colleagues whose personalities don't mesh with yours, just as there will be people who feel the same towards you—much like in your future working world. Loving in the short haul means learning to resolve conflicts in ways that are productive and fair to both parties. If you "stuff" your negative feelings, no one, including yourself, receives love. Sometimes it's startling to find how self-centered our natural instincts are. College offers practice in developing unselfish actions.

Loving your neighbor on campus can get tricky, though. One path to academic failure comes from saying yes to everyone who wants your friendship the moment they ask.

Tony understands this well. A tall, sandy-haired soccer player, he was voted "Best Personality" in high school. The very gifts of friendship he developed there worked against him in college. A constant stream of friends dropped into his dorm every night. "I probably studied at the most, a casual hour every day." When new friends invited him to skip class in favor of five-dollar ski days, the mountains and social life pulled him away from his studies. Pizza runs, playoffs on TV, party time—and a 1.5 fall semester—all this combined to make the friendliest freshman become the nonexistent sophomore.

Figuring out the balance between the planned and the serendipitous moments with friends on campus and academics takes experience—everyone is different.

But for most college students, the finest side-benefit of a college education is the lifelong friendships that emerge from living, laughing, working, studying together. Surprise friendships emerge—people with very different backgrounds and personalities mesh in delightful ways. If you're fortunate, international students attend your campus and usually welcome genuine overtures of friendship. Volunteer experiences in the community also expand one's sense of "who is my neighbor." You'll like far more people than you'll probably even have time to know well.

We can each bring to our neighbor the spirit that Paul spoke of in 1 Corinthians 13: Love bears all things (don't be surprised by the selfishness in yourself or your neighbor); believes all things (and looks always for the best in others); hopes all things (and lives thoughtfully with their future in mind); endures all things (and is guided by a spirit of forgiveness).

"Loving your neighbor" led Martin Luther King, Jr., into creative confrontation with his Southern citizens; moved Mother

Teresa into the slums of Calcutta; brought Millard Fuller around the world to start Habitat for Humanity houses; caused Julian to listen each day to the hearts of her Norwich neighbors; and surprised all of God's rare beasts on other unique adventures. Where will it lead you?

━━━━━━━━━

Loving Your Neighbor

And now these three remain: faith, hope and love.
But the greatest of these is love.

Love is patient,
Love is kind.
It does not envy,
It does not boast,
It is not proud.
It is not rude,
it is not self-seeking,
it is not easily angered,
it keeps no record of wrongs.
Love does not delight in evil
but rejoices with the truth.
It always protects,
always trusts,
always hopes,
always perseveres.

Love never fails.

—1 Corinthians 13:13, 4–8◻

Church: The Gathered Family ◙

For busy students, deciding to attend church on Sunday is a bit like deciding not to be sexually active—you need to know ahead of time what you plan to do. Most college environments do very little to encourage church attendance, and if you don't have an alarm clock and transportation, it's far more convenient to get some rest—some much needed rest.

So why go?

Christ's clear invitation is into a community of believers. Faith is not just a vertical relationship between God and humans; it's a horizontal expression of love from one person to another—"the church for others," as Bonhoeffer called it.

The local church is a testing ground—a gathering place for people of all ages and personalities. What is worship? "I need it," says Wendy, a senior. "It's a conscious reminder once a week to live out my priority of trying to put God first. That's easy to forget in college."

In many ways, the typical college campus sends out messages that are the opposite of the church's central beliefs. For example:

On Campus:	In Church:
Grades determine status	Apply your heart to wisdom
You determine your destiny	The human mind plans the way, but the Lord directs the steps (Proverbs 16:9)
Take charge	Follow me
Cultivate a critical spirit	Make me to hear joy and gladness
Make money	Some people, eager for money, have wandered from the faith and pierced themselves with many griefs (1 Timothy 6:10)

Worship, that public act of honoring God, helps us to remember that God has many people, with a variety of talents, to serve. Sometimes the most sensitive, caring college students try to wear the world on their shoulders, as if all its ills were theirs to solve. But Paul, in addressing the Corinthian church, states: "Now there are different kinds of gifts, but the same Spirit. There are different kinds of service, but the same Lord" (1 Corinthians 12:4). Throughout chapter 12, Paul continues to emphasize the importance of appreciating the individual talents that are gathered together in the body of believers. With such different gifts, none of us can cherish inflated ideas of our own importance. And beyond our own communities, there is an international community of the faithful that tries to be God's hands and feet in their own sphere of influence.

This global community has proven to be a vital force, cutting across all boundaries in their common sense of family. Somtimes they are a confrontive force in shaping a more just society; sometimes they are a healing force in restoring a broken world. Behind most major headlines during 1989 and 1990, the church played a role. When the wall came tumbling down in Berlin, East German pastors and lay people were asked to lead in the delicate post-wall negotiations. "They were the one group in the communist society experienced in democratic procedures," claimed Dr.

Darell Guder, who leads student exchanges to Berlin. For years a group called the Berlin Fellowship maintained contacts with Christians throughout Eastern Europe, traveling from America and West Germany to provide encouragement to Christians in the Eastern bloc. Issues of justice in Latin America continue to be brought before the U.S. Senate and Congress by concerned Catholic and Protestant church members who visit these war-torn countries. Black South African church leaders, along with some whites, draw on the international religious community to continue pressuring for the end of apartheid. And local church communities often provide shelter and food for America's growing homeless population. "Once you were not a people, but now you are the people of God; once you had not received mercy, but now you have received mercy," says the apostle Peter (1 Peter 2:10).

But also the full range of human nature—the good, the bad, and the ugly—is found in the community. Just as the church can be a powerful force for good, so historically the church also has misused its power to oppress, either through overt acts such as the Inquisition or the Crusades, or by acts of omission, like tacitly siding with an evil status quo or ignoring the sufferings of the masses.

Many thinking men and women find in these problems a reason to avoid what they consider a hypocritical church. The late British author Malcolm Muggeridge found inspiration in his interviews with Mother Teresa, and he candidly told her of his spiritual struggles with the imperfect church. She responded in a letter:

> Christ is longing to be your Food. Surrounded with fullness of loving food you allow yourself to starve. The personal love Christ has for you is infinite; the small difficulty you have regarding His church is finite. Overcome the finite with the infinite. Christ has created you because He wanted you. I know what you feel—terrible longing with dark emptiness. And yet He is the One in love with you.

The value of church often directly relates to our level of involvement. It is similar to what John F. Kennedy said in his inauguration address: "Ask not what your country [or church] can do for you, but ask what you can do for your country [or church]."

Church participation often opens some very unexpected doors. When a former fireman started teaching Sunday school to little kids, he learned how gifted he was with children. So at twenty-four, he decided to attend college to get a teaching degree. One young woman saw how much her singing moved an audience; now she is receiving professional voice training at the University of Colorado's prestigious music program in jazz and opera. A science student spent a summer in Haiti through a church mission program and found compelling reasons to go to medical school.

If you attended church with your family while growing up, college offers an excellent time to visit a variety of America's churches with their richly different traditions. Then, if you choose to become involved, choose one that represents your own commitments. If you never spent much time in church, don't miss experiencing this visible expression of the household of the Living God. There's music, toddlers, grandmas and grandpas, friends outside the college circle, a world vision, and the Word lifted up—all in an hour on Sunday morning. Why not set the alarm? ▣

Champion Givers ◙

It is more blessed to give than to receive.   ACTS 20:35

God loves a cheerful giver.   2 CORINTHIANS 9:7

The ability to cultivate a generous spirit in college often conflicts with the economic pressures of scraping together enough money for tuition, books, housing, food—basics in earning an education. But being short of money forces us to think of resourceful ways to give of ourselves—drawing closer to the heart of God's desire for generous spirits.

In spring of 1989, the Gonzaga University baseball team learned this firsthand from Soviet young people. The team traveled thousands of miles from Spokane, Washington, to share their skills with baseball players in Tbilisi, the capital city of the Republic of Georgia in the Soviet Union.

For days, the Georgians enthusiastically learned the rudiments of American baseball—fielding ground balls, hitting the curve, stealing bases, even chewing Copenhagen. After returning to their Spokane Jesuit school, the American students told John Blanchette, a sportswriter with *The Spokesman-Review,* their hometown newspaper, what they had learned in return. "They are at the junior-high level, but they love the game like we do. We have so much compared to them," said catcher, Dave Rypien. "But they'd give you anything they had. They are champion givers."

Nowhere did they see that more than at the final banquet, a humbling testimony to their hosts' generous spirits. One Georgian player bore a gift for the American coach, Steve Hertz. "His family home had been burned in a fire," Hertz explained. "Their treasure had been their library. He gave us a book, *The Knight in the Panther's Skin,* a very famous Georgian story, that was charred on the edges. Inside was written, 'To my American coach from your Georgian pupil.' It was the only book that had survived the fire."

Every day I see students give in unusually generous ways—even on limited budgets. Sometimes it's a gift of time: dropping their homework to critique another's paper, getting up early to bake birthday biscuits for a surprise breakfast in bed. Often it's a gift of encouragement: listening to a friend's feelings after a D minus or supporting a friend in a varsity game in the rain. Sometimes it's economic: raising money for a Habitat for Humanity project, or repairing a friend's car.

Would someone describe you as a champion giver? Or do you use lack of money as an excuse for a stingy spirit? Is there someone who needs a gift of your time, your talents, or your thoughtful words? ◼

Bigotry:
A Campus Disease ◘

*If I sit down at an empty table in the dining room, no
other students join me. They'll actually pick up an extra
chair from my table to join their American friends.*
                                AN AFRICAN EXCHANGE STUDENT

*Do nothing out of selfish ambition or vain conceit, but in
humility consider others better than yourselves. Each of you
should look not only to your own interests, but also to the
interests of others.*   PHILIPPIANS 2:3

Are you aware of students on your campus who feel
lonely and alienated because of prejudice? Across America, bigotry
poisons college campuses, creating tension and pain that hurt
humans to their core. The Carnegie Foundation report *Campus
Life: In Search of Community* paints a clear picture: The "idyllic
vision of college life often masks disturbing realities," including
racism, sexism, homophobia, and anti-Semitism.

No campus is immune. A *Time* magazine article on May 7,
1990, reports that, according to the Baltimore-based National
Institute Against Prejudice and Violence, since 1986 more than 250
colleges and universities, including top schools such as Brown,
Smith, and Stanford, have reported racist incidents, ranging from
swastikas painted on the walls to violent attacks and death threats
against specific people:

> Virtually every minority group finds itself under fire. For
> blacks, the trigger is often affirmative action: whatever their
> backgrounds or abilities, black students may find themselves
> viewed as beneficiaries of lowered standards. Asian students
> are attacked for the opposite reason—for "curve busting"

on grade scales and raising the level of competition for jobs in such fields as math, science, and engineering.

In the case of gays and lesbians, fear of AIDS has brought homophobia out of the closet: of 1,411 reports of gay-bashing on college campuses in 1988, 227 were classified as AIDS related. If students trust you, they may tell you of the ways it occurs on your own campus: from little slights to large scars. For international students, these incidents add to the aloneness they already feel. As one young man from Liberia explained, "The moment people hear I'm from Africa, the conversation seems to stop. This even happens when I meet black Americans." Another international student, whose second language is English, was asked "Can you count?" when she applied to work in a post office. "I felt like screaming . . . of course I can count; I'm in college!" During a spring filled with racial tensions at one East Coast university, racial epitaphs were smeared inside the Malcolm X house.

Universities aren't alone. According to *Time* magazine,

> An epidemic of ethnic hatred is sweeping the world, dismaying fair-minded people who are at a loss to explain it. Why are Jewish cemeteries in France and Italy being desecrated? Why are Turks in Bulgaria and Koreans in Japan viewed as infections in the national bloodstream? Why do Africa's Hutu and Tutsi tribes continue to slaughter one another? The core of the problem seems to be the determination of almost every group to feel superior to others.

Many observers feel that college campuses simply mirror the tension in the society around them. When students converge on a campus, they've often never even known someone from another culture.

But prejudice is seen in more than just racial issues. Even in some Christian colleges, students report that the fervently Christian students can sometimes dominate other groups by their smug sense of superiority. "As a Hindu, I felt that students only wanted to tell me about their God and their Bible," observed a student from India, "but they showed no interest in understanding my sense of God or our holy scriptures."

Often the problem is simply a culturally ingrained ignorance. For this reason many campuses have initiated international-awareness weeks with multi-cultural workshops and curriculum changes to heighten awareness and understanding of other cultures. Faculties, administrators, and staff, as well as students, attend these. Listening is the first step to knowing what we're doing or saying that hurts another.

At Davidson College in North Carolina, a group of students calling themselves "The Bathroom Brigade for Geographical Literacy" posted world maps in all the bathroom stalls after placement tests showed many college students couldn't even identify major countries. "It's an easy way to learn, and the maps can't be ignored," said a college spokesperson. It's a first step.

The Bible offers Jesus as a model of how we should relate to one another—so that no human or group feels superior to another. In Philippians 2:5–8, Paul says,

> *Your attitude should be the same as that of Jesus Christ:*
> *Who, being in very nature God,*
> *did not consider equality with God*
> *something to be grasped,*
> *but made himself nothing,*
> *taking the very nature of a servant,*
> *being made in human likeness.*
> *And being found in appearance as a man,*
> *he humbled himself*
> *and became obedient to death—*
> *even death on a cross!*

For Christians wanting to follow the radical attitude of Jesus, every person has importance and worth. If Christ, who didn't feel superior while being equal to God, chose the road of humility, there's no room for human superiority. But even in adopting this attitude, it takes humility for us to admit that we all harbor remnants of cultural prejudice. Learning about these during college-sponsored workshops may be the first chance to see how even words or acts can unintentionally hurt others.

Students, faculty, and staff who break through these barriers and earn the trust of a person from another culture are given a glimpse into the heart of another's world. You don't have to travel

LOVING YOUR NEIGHBOR

abroad to gain this rich experience; just become a friend to someone on campus.

Are all your friends from backgrounds similar to yours? Why? Why not take a small step today to be a friend to someone new? The kindness of one person can ease the bigotry of another. You can be a healing agent to counter the cruel moments of campus life. And most likely you'll discover that a friend is a gift you give yourself.■

A Helping Hand ▣

Now let us do something beautiful for God!
MOTHER TERESA

Kindness is a language that the blind can see and the deaf can hear.
ANONYMOUS

Often students give their time to volunteer work, sometimes for a few hours a week, sometimes for more. Students at Seattle Pacific University volunteer with NightWatch, a group that helps find shelter for the homeless; Westmont College sponsors Potter's Clay, in which athletes use their spring break to build homes and play sports with children in Mexico; at Yale, students help local immigrants learn English.

Jon, a senior in education, spent a term in cross-cultural study in Antigua, Guatemala. To meet his education requirement, he volunteered to help in the Hermano Pedro orphanage, a Catholic home that specializes in caring for handicapped children. It is an unusually cheerful environment, where little ones wake up with a sense of security and joy in spite of their troubled lives. Bright, colorful pictures adorn the adobe walls, Christmas trees add their charm, beautiful gardens offer a sense of peace within the courtyard walls. The staff brings a sense of warmth and professionalism, although health care, cleanliness, and food service take up most of their time.

When Jon first arrived, the needs overwhelmed him. "What can I do in just three hours a day for four weeks?" he wondered. On the second day, he noticed Anelicia, a tiny two-year-old toddler—only she didn't toddle. Originally brought in with spinal meningitis, which also caused deafness, she was so sick it had taken months to restore any strength in her at all. Even then she spent most of her time in an infant seat because the muscles in her legs were not strong enough to crawl.

Jon decided to teach her to crawl. Each morning, he would lift the smiling girl out of her seat and place her on the floor with a toy slightly out of reach. Then the six-foot rugby player would get down on all fours and try to demonstrate to Anelicia how to move her tiny arms and legs in a crawling motion. Soon the bright girl, eyes aglow, started to try. "Her spirit and effort astounded me," said Jon. "We'd work for twenty or thirty minutes, then she'd be exhausted, so we'd break for a while. Then we'd start again."

By the end of four weeks, Anelicia could scoot all over the floor, traveling up to thirty feet! "It may not make sense to others, but seeing her beautiful smile and excitement at being able to move feels like the greatest success I've ever had." Like most volunteer experiences, Jon's helped him reap rewards far beyond his imagination. A superb athlete, he left with a new respect for the fortune of having a healthy body, and as a future teacher, he now understands the need for patience. But more than this, he is linked in love with a Guatemalan child. Not bad for four weeks of volunteer work!

Have you considered carving out a few hours each week or month to serve in your community? Getting off campus— meeting others outside the college environment and learning about human needs first hand—inevitably adds adventure to your education. And it gives hands and feet to the command "Love one another." What's holding you back? ▣

Shipwreck
and Survival □

An oak puts deeper roots because of storms ...
ANONYMOUS

*Shipwreck is the coming apart of what has served as
shelter and protection and has held and carried one where
one wanted to go—the collapse of a structure that once
promised trustworthiness.* EDUCATOR SHARON PARKS

Do you have friends who try to cope with college
while wading through murky emotional waters? During any
given term, many students find their lives torn apart by surprise
sorrows: parental divorce; family financial failure; breaking of
significant relationships; death of moms, dads, family members,
and friends; suicides; parental abandonment. It can feel like
"shipwreck"—a term used by theologian Richard Niebuhr to
describe the unraveling of what has held a person's world together.

Jeff remembers this sense of emotional sabotage. When he
hauled his bags up the staircase to his dorm at the start of his
freshman year, he was full of confidence. Moving was no big deal.
The son of an Army man, he had changed schools eleven times
and always found a quick niche because of his exceptional baseball
skills. Nothing could have prepared him for the Thanksgiving
news that changed him from a carefree, confident person to, as he
put it, "an inconsistent, angry, confused" young man.

The morning after arriving home for break, his parents called
him into their bedroom. His mother's voice was soft and faltering.
She told him, "Your dad has melanoma cancer. The doctors say
it's terminal. He has one to six months."

"I couldn't believe what I heard," he told me later, "and I just
started to cry. My folks had chosen to wait to tell me in person.

Dad's greatest concern was for his kids—my younger brother, my sister, and me."

His parents said they wanted Jeff to return to school and finish his semester. Although he did, he felt alienated. "Taking finals suddenly seemed so trivial. Everyone was in this Christmas spirit, and I was just bitter. The world seemed like a cruel place."

One afternoon, Jeff felt like his whole world was exploding. "I was feeling guilty. As the oldest in the family, I thought I should be home. I leaned against the closet in my room, slumped down, and started to scream and cry, 'Why, God? Why? It's not fair—he's only thirty-nine!' My roommate came in, kneeled down beside me, and was really comforting. He knew how to listen without trying to give answers."

Jeff stumbled through finals, went home, and spent his Christmas holidays in the hospital, trying to comfort his dad—and his mom. On January 3, his dad died. After staying home with his mom in January, he returned to college for spring semester.

When melting snow finally gives way to the greening of campus, an exuberance breaks out in students. It's a zany, rambunctious time, with stereos blasting through open windows, frisbees flying everywhere, and couples and groups dotting the lawns, studying, sunning, and enjoying life. But Jeff felt only grief. "I spent the spring pretending. I'd say to people, 'Yeah, I'm okay.' But I was incredibly inconsistent and moody. Most of the time I just wanted to be alone. My girlfriend would ask what I wanted and I didn't know. All I really wanted was my dad back."

The one person with whom Jeff could be honest was the dorm chaplain. Every Thursday afternoon, he would visit Jeff's room just to talk and sometimes pray. "His presence was so soothing. I couldn't handle much organized religion at the time." His roommate also helped by inviting him to pickup games in baseball. "We'd have a fun time. But mainly I was just angry. I couldn't wait for the semester to end so I could go home."

The next year brought the beginning of rebuilding, but when Jeff packed his belongings and walked down the stairs of his dorm at the end of his freshman year, he was simply a survivor of shipwreck.

Sometimes it's confusing to know when to give a person "space" and when to come alongside. Paul tells the Philippians: "How good of you to share in my troubles." But grief cannot be rushed and perhaps Jeff hints at the highest kindness when he talks of his friend who listened and prayed and didn't try to give quick or trite answers. There is a famous prayer commonly attributed to St. Francis that speaks about the kind of friend who stands alongside people going through shipwreck.

> Lord, make me an instrument of thy peace;
> Where there is hatred, let me sow love;
> Where there is injury, pardon;
> Where there is doubt, faith;
> Where there is despair, hope;
> Where there is darkness, light;
> Where there is sadness, joy.
>
> O divine Master, grant that I may not so much seek
> To be consoled as to console,
> To be understood as to understand,
> To be loved as to love;
> For it is in giving that we receive;
> It is in pardoning that we are pardoned;
> It is in dying [to self] that we are born to eternal life. ▣

The Star Thrower ◘

Blessed is he who has regard for the weak. PSALM 41:1

Nobody made a greater mistake than he who did nothing because he could only do a little.
ENGLISH PHILOSOPHER EDMUND BURKE

Has a simple event ever made you change the way you think or feel about something? Just such a moment happened to Loren Eisely, the great naturalist, during one of his pre-dawn walks on the seaside of Costabel. Plagued by insomnia, he often got up early to walk the beach. Each sunrise he saw the townspeople combing the sand for starfish to kill for commercial purposes. For Eisely it was a sign, however small, of all the ways the world says no to life.

But one morning Eisely got up unusually early, well before the crowds arrived, and discovered a solitary figure on the beach. This man was also gathering starfish, but each time he found one alive he would pick it up and throw it far into the breaking surf, back to the nurturing ocean. As days went by, Eisely found this man embarked on his mission of mercy each morning, seven days a week, no matter what the weather.

Eisely named him the "star thrower," and in a moving meditation he wrote of how this man and his pre-dawn work contradicted everything Eisely had been taught about evolution and the survival of the fittest. Here on the beach in Costabel, the strong reached down to save, not crush, the weak. And Eisely wondered, "Is there a star thrower at work in the universe, a God whose nature (in the words of Thomas Merton) is 'mercy within mercy within mercy'?"

Parker Palmer, a contemporary Quaker writer, tells this "star thrower" story in an article, suggesting how rich it is with meaning: "It offers an image of a God who threw the stars and throws them still." It speaks of how ordinary men and women can participate in "God's enveloping mercy. It suggests a vocation that each of us could undertake: to recognize, to identify and lift up those moments, those acts, those people, those stories that contradict the ways in which the world says no to life."

This story shows that each person can make a difference. To the cynic who asks, "Does it make any difference if a few starfish are thrown back?" the person who believes our actions matter answers, "Well, it does to the starfish."

Star throwers come in all shapes and sizes—often beautifully unaware how their actions affect others. Some acts of kindness can secretly travel continents away. A visiting Chinese language professor, steeped in Communist thought and tradition, became curious about Americans and the Christian faith through a seemingly unimportant event. One day he was leading a group of American church members on a tour of the Great Wall of China. "While we climbed the wall, one of the young men picked up litter along the way—a simple act to clean up the environment. I'd been so conditioned to believe negative things about Christians, his act startled me. I began to wonder if all I'd been told was true." The young man's act led the professor to search for understanding himself, which is why he decided to choose a church-related college while studying in the United States.

Another small anonymous act gave Ginetta Sagan, a young Italian woman, a will to live. After she had been jailed and tortured by the Nazis during World War II, a stranger threw into her prison cell a matchbox on which was written the word *corigga*—courage. "At a pivotal moment," she explained, "it let me know someone cared if I survived." This act of encouragement eventually led to her becoming a founding member of Amnesty International in the U.S. to offer similar hope to other prisoners of conscience.

Student star throwers abound, and their acts shape the world in ways they seldom know. Each letter a student writes on behalf of a political prisoner adopted by Amnesty International is a tangible act with an intangible result—an act of hope. When Bishop Tutu spoke at Wesleyan University in Connecticut in spring of 1990, he thanked the students throughout America who had fought for divestment in South Africa. In his tribute, he stated, "The time students gave showed they cared about justice, not just their grades or the rat race. Because of this, Mandela is free. Because of economic sanctions, the South African government is learning that freedom is cheaper than repression. Your acts have made a difference."

Student initiatives on environmental issues are causing many campuses to organize recycling programs.

Are you—or would you like to be—a star thrower? ◼

Mother Teresa: Giver of Joy ◙

It will be for posterity to decide if [Mother Teresa] is a saint. I can only say of her that in a dark time she is a burning and a shining light; in a cruel time, a living embodiment of Christ's gospel of love; in a godless time, the Word dwelling among us, full of grace and truth.

ENGLISH WRITER MALCOLM MUGGERIDGE

The Work is his Work and will remain so; all of us are but his instruments, who do our little bit and pass by.

MOTHER TERESA

One Star Thrower, Mother Teresa, known as "the saint of the gutters," received the Nobel Peace Prize in 1979. But when she began her pioneer work with the "poorest of the poor" by establishing homes for abandoned children and dying derelicts in the streets of Calcutta, India, critics sometimes questioned the insignificant scale of her work compared to the enormous needs. That never stopped her or the Sisters of Charity. "Christian love isn't about numbers, it's about a person." And clearly it makes a difference to the abandoned people now in the sister's joyful care.

One day in 1946, Teresa, a Yugoslavian nun working in India, received "the call within a call" while riding the train to Darjeeling. "I heard the call to give up all and follow him into the slums to serve him among the poorest of the poor. I knew it was his will and that I had to follow him." After receiving permission from Pope Pius XII, she left the lovely Loreto convent where she had taught, took some training in medical work, and then moved to the most wretched quarter of Calcutta. She gathered together five homeless children and began her ministry of love.

LOVING YOUR NEIGHBOR

Since then her work has multiplied throughout the world. Missionaries of Charity now have homes in fifty Indian cities, Australia, Latin America, Italy, Tanzania, Sri Lanka, Jordon, Venezuela, and the United States (where she has helped found homes for AIDS victims)—over thirty countries in all.

Malcolm Muggeridge, in his excellent book about Mother Teresa, called *Something Beautiful for God*, tells her story in vivid detail. He visited and interviewed her over several months and quotes her extensively. What most astonished him, and others who have visited one of the many established homes, was the spirit of joy that the sisters showed.

Included here are just a few of her thoughts:

On Love of God: "Thou shalt love the Lord thy God with thy whole heart, with thy whole soul and with thy whole mind." This is the commandment of the great God and he cannot command the impossible. Love is a fruit in season at all times and within reach of every hand. Anyone may gather it and no limit is set. Everyone can reach this love through meditation, spirit of prayer and sacrifice, by an intense inner life.

On Prayer: Prayer enlarges the heart until it is capable of containing God's gift of himself. Ask and seek, and your heart will grow big enough to receive him and keep him as your own.

On Joy: She gives most who gives with joy. The best way to show our gratitude to God and the people is to accept everything with joy. A joyful heart is the normal result of a heart burning with love.

On Kindness: Be kind and merciful. Let no one ever come to you without coming away better and happier. Be the living expression of God's kindness: kindness in your face, kindness in your eyes, kindness in your smile, kindness in your warm greeting.

On Silence: We need to find God, and he cannot be found in noise and restlessness. God is the friend of silence. See how nature, trees, flowers, grass grow in silence; see the stars, the moon and sun, how they move in silence. Is not our mission to give God to the poor in the slums? Not a dead God, but a living, loving God. The more we receive in silent prayer, the more we can give in active life. We need silence to be able to touch souls.

On Need: The biggest disease today is not leprosy or tuberculosis, but rather the feeling of being unwanted, uncared for and deserted by everybody. The greatest evil is the lack of love and charity, the terrible indifference towards one's neighbor who lives at the roadside assaulted by exploitation, corruption, poverty and disease.◘

LOVING
YOUR
SELF

Introduction:
The Essential
Command ◼

A simple Russian country priest was confronted by an eminent scientist who gave devastating arguments against the existence of God. Then he declared, "I don't believe in God." The unlettered priest retorted quickly, "Oh, it doesn't matter—God believes in you." BISHOP DESMOND TUTU

I find it interesting that Jesus and modern psychologists agree that loving our neighbor is closely linked to loving ourselves. But what does it mean to love ourselves?

It differs from narcissism—that excessive preoccupation with ourselves that critics say characterized the "me generation." On any campus, signs of narcissism abound. Students devote hours to sculpting perfect bodies in the weight room; the frantic pursuit of the 4.0; volunteerism simply to "résumé build." These are all ways people love themselves by looking out for Number One.

But rarely do these students genuinely love themselves. External success often hides an internal sense of inadequacy, masking such feelings as: "I need a perfect body to be loved"; "Unless I achieve superior grades, I'm not okay"; "Without a stunning résumé no one will want to hire me." But is there another way to love ourselves?

Yes! It starts by accepting Christ's unconditional love. "We love because he first loved us" (1 John 4:19). It's unearned; changeless; forever. And our Creator never abandons us. Yet it's hard to love yourself if you haven't felt sustained with unconditional, predictable love. Any first-grade teacher can point out the children who seemed "loved." At ease with themselves, they're able to enjoy and reach out to others. The idea of a loving God would seem natural to these children.

But in America, where many college students experience alienation in their homes—either through broken relationships or preoccupied parents—the tendency for self-rejection is common. What makes this lack of self-love even more painful is that we really are all selfish—something we all know firsthand. Sin abounds—which shouldn't surprise us—but our feelings of inadequacy and guilt often keep us from believing and feeling we are lovable. A shameful action can run over and over in our minds—spiraling our sense of separation from a holy God.

Although her language may sound strange to our twentieth-century ears, Julian of Norwich wrote about this same problem back in the twelfth century:

> Our courteous Lord does not want his servants to despair because they fall often and grievously; for our falling does not hinder him in loving us. Peace and love are always in us, living and working, but we are not always in peace and love. . . . No more than his love towards us is withdrawn because of our sin does he wish our love to be withdrawn from ourselves or from our fellow Christians.

There's a vivid scene in one of Maya Angelou's books, *Singin' and Swingin' and Gettin' Merry Like Christmas,* that demonstrates the kind of despair Julian of Norwich spoke about. Angelou is a contemporary writer (who also appeared, by the way, as Kunte Kinte's grandmother in the television drama *Roots*). In one passage, Maya describes her struggle when she became convinced she had been a terrible mother to her young son. A single parent, having given birth to her son out of wedlock, she was also a talented singer and dancer. When she joined the international touring company of *Porgy and Bess,* which traveled to Africa, her young son, left with her family, went into such distress at her absence that he broke out in hives. When Maya returned, she was beside herself with guilt.

She even started to feel suicidal and fear she was going crazy, so she tried to see a white psychiatrist. Unable to talk, she walked out and went to a close friend she calls Uncle Wilkie:

LOVING YOURSELF

"Wilkie, I can't see any reason for living. I went to a psychiatrist and it was no good. I couldn't talk. I'm so unhappy. And I have done so much harm to Clyde. . . ."

He held me until I finished my babbling.

"Are you finished?" His voice was stern and unsympathetic.

I said, "Well, I guess so."

"Sit down at that desk. Now see that yellow tablet? See that pencil? Now write down what you have to be thankful for."

"Wilkie, I don't want silly answers."

"Start to write." His voice was cold and unbending. "And I mean start now! First, write that you heard me tell you that. So you have the sense of hearing. And that you could tell the taxi driver where to bring you and then tell me what was wrong with you, so you have the sense of speech. You can read and write. You have a son who needs nothing but you. Write, dammit! I mean write."

I picked up the pencil and began.

I can hear.

I can speak.

I have a son.

I have a mother.

I have a brother.

I can dance.

I can sing.

I can cook.

I can read.

I can write.

When I reached the end of the page I began to feel silly. I was alive and healthy. What on earth did I have to complain about? For two months in Rome I had said all I wanted was to be with my son. And now I could hug and kiss him anytime the need arose. What the hell was I whining about?

Wilkie said, "Now write, 'I am blessed. And I am grateful.'" When he walked me to the door he put his arm around my shoulders. "Maya, you're a good mother. If you weren't, Clyde wouldn't have missed you so much.

"And let Uncle Wilkie tell you one last thing. Don't ask God to forgive you, for that's already done. Forgive yourself. You're the only person you can forgive. You've done nothing wrong. So forgive yourself."

Uncle Wilkie understood the heart of what it means to love ourselves. He wanted Maya to go out into the world again in "peace and love." Martin Luther King, Jr., stated, "Forgiveness is not a one time act; it's a permanent attitude." To love ourselves means to daily forgive ourselves, and then we're free also to forgive others.

It also means accepting and believing in ourselves, and like Maya—naming specifically our talents and gifts. Then, with a thankful spirit, we need to let our imagination soar while considering the future.

But loving yourself is more than an attitude—it's an action. No longer under the roof of a mom and dad who helped provide care, loving yourself means taking care of yourself. It means seeing to all the mundane but vital things—like getting enough sleep, eating healthy foods, seeing doctors when needed, avoiding substance abuse, respecting your sexuality. Neglect even one of these areas and eventually the whole body and emotions can be torn apart.

And take time alone to know yourself. One of the great risks of college is that when you're bombarded with so much, it's hard to find time alone to think. But time needs to be carved out and fought for and valued. If you can be gentle with yourself and take the same kind of time to listen to your interior voice as the exterior voices that clamor for attention, you will hear that "still small voice" of the Spirit. "You are loved . . . and nothing—absolutely nothing—can separate you from the love of Christ."

As Paul says in Romans 8:38–39, "I am convinced that neither death nor life, neither angels nor demons, neither the present nor the future, nor any powers, neither height nor depth, nor anything else in all creation, will be able to separate us from the love of God that is in Christ Jesus our Lord."◙

Alcohol Abuse ◙

Wine is a mocker and beer a brawler; whoever is led astray by them is not wise.   PROVERBS 20:1

I get really confused and angry when I see friends in the dorm get smashed every Friday and Saturday night and then act like such devoted church-goers on Sunday morning. They seem like fly-by-night Christians.
          A NEW STUDENT AT A CHURCH-RELATED COLLEGE

The use and abuse of alcohol is as much a part of every campus as taking classes. The only difference is: Drinking is not a prerequisite.

You may wonder. "Heavy drinking, or at least some drinking of alcoholic beverages, is something that everybody does here," stated a student from the University of Miami in a *New York Times* article in March of 1990. "That's what being a college student is all about. Anyone who doesn't participate is stereotyped as someone who doesn't belong."

Sound like a familiar, even if unspoken, truth? The prevalence of alcohol and the opportunity for its abuse will be one of the first choices to confront you on any campus. Don't be misled into thinking it will be any different at a church-related college—in fact, it can be even worse because many students may be rebelling against parental values.

Despite the fact that twenty-one is the legal drinking age in all fifty states—and despite the tightening of alcohol policies on almost every campus—surveys show that most college students continue to drink regularly and often heavily. The University of Michigan's tenth annual national survey from the Institute of Social Research shows heavy binge drinking has not changed much over recent years. In 1989, over 41 percent of students drank five or more drinks in two weeks; 76 percent had at least one drink in thirty days.

Alcohol is clearly the drug of choice on campuses around the country. Misled by their ability to drink heavily without apparent effect, many abusive student drinkers of today become tomorrow's alcoholics.

But in the past decade, more students have chosen to drink in moderation. The influence of MADD, Mothers Against Drunk Driving, and high-school and college organizations committed to teaching responsible drinking is altering the climate of opinion, especially in regard to the necessity of always having designated drivers.

Some students claim there's plenty of opportunity to say no. "If you say you don't want to drink, you don't have to," says one Princeton senior. "It's not forced on you." Varsity athletes with high performance goals sometimes go through a season without alcohol or caffeine or cocaine to keep at the peak of their physical fitness. Another group of students, from alcoholic homes, knows the daily destruction alcohol does to lives. They recognize their own vulnerability to addiction and simply refuse to drink.

Many students say they later regret what happened when they were under the influence. "Alcohol became my great justifier of situational ethics," stated one senior soccer player. "Many of my actions I wouldn't have dreamed of doing while sober." One young woman, who got drunk at a friend's house while his parents were out of town, woke up in his bed in the middle of the night. "I was throwing up and all he could think of was—'Get out of here; you're going to stain my folks' carpet.'"

Research shows that campus crime is often linked to drugs and alcohol. An article in the January 17 issue of the *Chronicle of Higher Education* reports on research done at Towson State University in Maryland. Undergraduates from colleges across the country were interviewed about campus crime, and more than half of those who acknowledged committing crimes on or near campus said they were intoxicated by drugs or alcohol at the time; as were nearly half of those who said they were crime victims of such things as sexual assault, armed robbery, theft, and vandalism.

"The lesson is: Know when to leave the party," said Dorothy Siegel, vice-president for student services at Towson State. "If there are drugs at a party or abuse of alcohol, there are going to be victims."

If you find yourself addicted to alcohol or drugs, seek help now. Almost every campus and community has resources to cope with the disease of alcoholism or drug addiction. But a person needs to acknowledge the problem. Also, if you have grown up in a home affected by alcohol, these same organizations—such as campus counseling centers or Alcoholics Anonymous—also provide support groups for adult children of alcoholics.

Two things we know from the biblical record: Christ provided wine for a wedding celebration—very fine wine; and drunkenness is condemned. Obviously, if you choose to drink, loving yourself and your neighbor means learning to drink responsibly. Anything less can hurt like hell. Ask any child from an alcoholic family or any victim of drunk driving or date rape.◙

Campus Down Times: An Energy Robber ▣

The only thing we can do is play on the one string we have, and that is our attitude ... I am convinced that life is 10% what happens to me and 90% how I react to it. And so it is with you ... we are in charge of our Attitudes. PASTOR AND WRITER CHARLES SWINDOLL

There is no new thing under the sun. ECCLESIASTES

An observant chaplain from Mills College in California addressed the female student body one February:

> The sophomore slump is made up of about equal parts of despondency and griping: griping about the college and all its works, despondency about one's own life, present and future. It shows itself in apathy toward classes, in petty bickerings in the halls, in complaints about the food, in bull sessions about "How many people are going to transfer out?" and "What's the use of being here anyway?" Most of this is not good for the mind or soul.... The problem arises year after year.

Sound familiar? The chaplain delivered these words on February 21, 1954—over thirty-five years ago! Yet isn't it true of many campuses today? The author of Ecclesiastes spoke the truth when he lamented that there is nothing new under the sun.

It seems as unfair to say all sophomores will slump as it is to say all seniors will shine, but there's some truth in it. What causes this gloom and the hypercritical attitude it spawns? Is it the reality, after all the pressure to "get in," that college isn't utopia—that the "viewbooks" only show the best pictures? Or the realization that dreams involve hard, daily, grinding work? That professors, roommates, cooks, and sports teams are abundantly human—with shortcomings that grate on us? Or confusion over "Why am I here?" especially if one hasn't chosen a major that provides a sense of purpose?

Does a mood of negativity ever predominate on your campus—like around mid-terms or in the harsh months of a cold winter? Why would a college chaplain say this grumbling is "not good for the mind or soul?" Sometimes this can become severe enough to affect your ability to function and work your best—and it can block your vision of the goodness in everyday life.

Creative students learn to take responsibility for their moods and attitudes. Heather, a senior who grew up on a farm, observed, "Sometimes the collective depressions weigh my spirits down, so I've discovered a way that almost always solves this." One evening, she figured this out by accident when she returned to the dorms after a long session of play practice. "My roommate and some other friends were in the hallway frowning and complaining about all they had to do. Homework was overwhelming—*two* five-page reports, a quiz, and about ten-hundred pages to read." Teachers were unreasonable: "They don't even consider that we have three other classes to study for. And the freshmen on our floor were too loud for us upperclass students to study."

"I was in a good mood from the comedy I had just been rehearsing, so I suggested, 'Well, let's all go to the HUB for an extra thick milkshake,' hoping that would pull them out of the bad mood. My roommate waved the idea away, 'We already did that.' The response knocked my high spirits to the basement. They'd already slurped down an extra-thick chocolate shake and they were *still* in this kind of mood? And worse yet, they'd gone without me. 'But you go on ahead, we don't want to drag you down.' Nice try, people, but it's a little late to tell me that. How am I supposed to be happy when my friends are all depressed?

So, Heather, who always enjoys the outdoors, took her jacket and quietly slipped into the cool spring night. Later she wrote about how she discovered a college coping skill. "I trudged along, unconsciously circling the loop while my thoughts grumbled in darkness. Then the overpoweringly sweet scent of blossoms cut through the clouds in my head as I stopped to look for the source. Next to the sidewalk I saw a golden forsythia, and fallen petals scattered the ground like sparks. A light wind whispered with the pines, discussing the coming of summer. I continued my walk with my head raised and mind open to the evening. Eventually I ended up at the top of the weeping birch next to the campanile. The breeze gently rocked my attitude completely around to the good."

Other students try other approaches: a quick pickup game of basketball, a drive alone in their car, rereading a favorite letter, playing music that lifts their spirits, or telephoning a close friend.

Heather didn't avoid facing genuine problems when they confronted her. But she learned to distinguish between those and the times when "prevailing negative winds," over problems she couldn't change, wrapped around the campus. She can't change the reality that pressure at mid-terms and finals will always exist; gray skies and icy streets last longer than anyone wants—but she can change how she lives within them. Do you know the difference?

O God,
Give us the serenity to accept what cannot be changed,
courage to change what should be changed,
and wisdom to distinguish the one from the other.
—Reinhold Niebuhr ▣

Loving Your
Sexual Self ▣

*So God created humankind in his image, in the image of
God he created them; male and female he created
them. . . . God saw everything that he had made, and
indeed, it was very good.*

GENESIS 1:27, 31 (NEW REVISED STANDARD VERSION)

*Each weekend after our games, we'd go to the largest
party in town, drink, find a friendly woman, and score
again. But you know, the next morning I always felt
crappy. I knew we just used one another to fulfill fifteen
minutes of gratification. I rarely saw the woman again.*

A FOOTBALL PLAYER

In an era of unprecedented freedom, college students
face difficult sexual choices. Some choose to forego the attractions
of instant intimacy and demonstrate a quiet confidence in
themselves. But they are a minority—almost an endangered
species. If surveys are to be believed, according to the National
Survey of Family Growth, seven out of ten teenagers are sexually
active by age eighteen. If men and women conform to the norms
of many campuses, there is pressure to be sexually active, even if
they commit very little to their relationships. Apart from one-night
stands, campus romances typically last about three months. Like a
good movie or dinner, sex becomes another weekend recreation.
Fun, but fleeting.

I've procrastinated in writing this chapter because students
express vastly different experiences and concerns. The nineteen-
year-old basketball player, who tells me his high-school girlfriend
is pregnant, confronts quite different issues than the senior woman

who is frustrated with the non-dating norms in the campus community.

Also, the level of sex education and discussion varies widely from campus to campus. Some colleges offer courses or seminars on human sexuality that explore the full dimensions of our sexual natures. Almost always, these are well attended. Other colleges simply emphasize "safe sex." Health educators at one prestigious East Coast university admonish their frosh: "You worked hard to get accepted here; don't blow it by getting pregnant." To insure this, students are required to attend health-education seminars that include passing a cucumber and condom around so students can practice correct protection. To aid in early detection, posters in bathroom stalls identify symptoms of sexually transmitted diseases and a phone number for testing services.

At some colleges, sex is a silent topic; they take an "each to his or her own" philosophy, offering few resources, information, or discussion. But such ignorance proves costly. In Whitman County in Washington State, home of a major university and several private colleges, sexually transmitted diseases have reached epidemic proportions, jeopardizing the future health and childbearing potential of many young adults. Chlamydia, which often goes undetected and can lead to sterility, is double the regional average.

But though experiences and environments vary, we all share a common bond in wanting to understand our sexual selves. From the beginning, the Bible affirms that God created us male and female with strong sexual desire—and it was good! Not only that, our inventive God designed our bodies for exceptional pleasure-giving intimacy and the miraculous gift of procreation. After all, we could have been created to rub feet or just collect spores! And in the context of committed love, people experience a profound sense of affirmation, emotional safety, and the wonder of being able to give birth to family.

The National Conference of Catholic Bishops recently established guidelines to teach human sexuality in schools and parishes. They describe our sexuality as a "wonderful gift," far more profound than any simple biological urge. Their 185-page document goes on to say, "Sexuality involves the whole person

174   LOVING YOURSELF

because it permeates all facets of the human personality: the physical, the psycho-emotional, the intellectual, the spiritual and ethical, and the social."

But if sex is so good, how did it get distorted? Today's casual sex has created a minefield. Does a sense of physical safety, affirmation, and joyful expectation of childbirth describe most campus sexual encounters? In our era of sexual freedom, dangers abound. It is a simple and necessary act of loving yourself to take a hard look at sexual norms around you and consider their price. As one older student asked a beautiful freshman who spontaneously slept with the man of the moment, "Have you ever considered you might be giving yourself away too easily?"

Many students, especially women, confess that casual sex has slowly eroded their self-esteem. "At first, I felt a surge of confidence," explains one woman, looking back on college. "But in changing partners, I was searching for intimacy and affection from men who weren't ready or wanting it, at least from me. By the end of college, my self-esteem plunged so low it took years to trust men again. I felt very vulnerable."

Other students claim their sexual activity hardly affects them at all—perhaps a sad commentary on twentieth-century resistance to attachment. As one young man said, "It's no big deal. It's healthy and feels good." Rather than an ultimate expression of faithfulness, commitment, or contentment, sexual encounters offer experimentation, power, and comparison.

But for victims of sexual violence, whether through childhood abuse or date rapes in college, the distortions of sex are devastating. One young woman, who had been sexually assaulted by a neighbor from the ages of eight to twelve, cried as she told me, "I'm so angry that something that happened so long ago still affects me every day. One of my professors even has the same smile, same eyes, and similar walk. I can hardly stand going into his class." Or consider the woman who was sexually assaulted at a fraternity party and pressed charges. What most devastated her was how the young men could so insensitively betray her trust. "Sure, I'd been drinking," she said. "But they were my buddies. I'd been like a little sister in the house. I couldn't believe they'd do this—and their denial of it all doubled the pain." As a symptom of the mentality of denial, college gang rapes are seldom called "rape," but rather, spectrums, ledging, beaching, or pulling train—a spectator sport for drinkers.

Our sexual choices reflect our inward beliefs about ourselves. Nothing is more intimate, more expressive, than giving our bodies to someone. For Christians wanting to live lives of commitment, the biblical imperative given to the early Christians in Rome offers much wisdom: "Do not conform any longer to the pattern of this world, but be transformed by the renewing of your mind. Then you will be able to test and approve what God's will is—his good, pleasing and perfect will" (Romans 12:2). It is a call to trust in the original blessing of sex—as an expression of loving commitment to a person, and a consistent courage not to conform to cultural norms. This includes loving our future selves, believing the words of God: " 'For I know the plans I have for you,' declares the Lord, 'Plans to prosper you and not to harm you, plans to give you hope and a future' " (Jeremiah 29:11).

To be "transformed by the renewing of your mind" includes knowing that college provides new beginnings. It's a time to think through the values you want to live out. High school patterns don't need to be adult choices. College offers exceptional friendships, in which openness in discussing our sexuality usually proves helpful. "Too many students come to college fearing sex," claims one senior male. "They treat it like alcohol—either binge or abstain, but they don't allow themselves to genuinely talk about it. In the dorm, their thoughts come out in crude, vulgar jokes, but that's just because they don't have another avenue of expression. But these are actually great years to listen to women and try to understand them and ourselves better."

The Bible also expresses a high view of the human body. Naturally, sexual temptation also existed in biblical days, and the advice was to "flee from sexual immorality. All other sins a man commits are outside his body, but he who sins sexually sins against his own body. Do you not know that your body is a temple of the Holy Spirit, who is in you, whom you have received from God? You are not your own; you were bought at a price. Therefore honor God with your body" (1 Corinthians 6:18).

College can provide the finest relationships one can experience. College fosters a closeness, especially now with co-ed dorms, that encourages lifelong friendships. Though sexual desires prove strong, living with healthy respect for oneself and other people, and resisting conformity to college sexual norms simply makes sense. It reflects confidence in God's good design, and it gives a lasting, not fleeting, freedom. "Be strong and of good courage," says our God.▣

A Twist
on Failure ▣

Some days I just feel like one big failure.
CONNIE, STUDENT BODY OFFICER WITH A 3.7 GRADE-
POINT

*In God's sight we do not fall, in our sight we do not
stand. As I see it both of these are true. But the deeper
insight belongs to God.* JULIAN OF NORWICH

In February of her junior year, Connie, a student leader, returned to campus to find her mailbox piled high with NSF (nonsufficient funds) slips from her bank and urgent letters from stores. The reason? During the pressure of finals and hurry of packing for home at Christmas, she hadn't balanced her checkbook carefully.

In all, five checks bounced—each with a $12.00 fee. "I felt so stupid!" she said. But when two of the checks bounced a second time, two stores turned her account over to collection agencies. "When I retraced my steps I found I'd originally made a $7.00 error. But with the $12.00 fee ... even my small $3.00 and $4.00 checks bounced. I was scared to death about my credit rating."

But the most embarrassing thing was having to call her parents for one of those "bail me out" pleas. "Actually, I thought my mom would be understanding, but she was really annoyed with my carelessness." But Connie did get help, and then called each store, apologized, and asked them to honor her original checks.

We shouldn't be too surprised with failure. In surveys of business executives, they often agree that failure proves the best teacher. It worked for Connie, who carefully keeps her accounts now.

Many professors understand this principle. At the University of Houston, Jack Matson, an engineering professor, offers an unusual class called Innovative Design for Civil Engineers, but affectionately dubbed "Failure 101" by students. From day one, he *wants* his students to *value* failure as an essential part in the creative learning process. The object of the course is to teach engineering students how to be innovative and entrepreneurial— encouraging students to take risks and be creative.

But this isn't easy for today's students—who are grilled from the beginning that only success matters. In an article in the *Chronicle of Higher Education,* Debra Blum described how professor Matson will come to class dressed crazily each day— maybe wearing a World War I combat helmet or a T-shirt of a two-legged chair with the word "Failure." Students often greet his costumes with a chorus of boos and thumbs-down gestures, which are actually signs of their approval. "My silly headgear is all part of the opposite mentality I'm trying to foster; it's meant to illustrate the importance of spontaneity and serendipity in life."

All of our lives we're taught that only success counts, but we have to recognize the role of failure in learning and creating too. "I'm not advocating failure for its own sake," explains Matson. "But there is something that I call 'intelligent failure' that provides the building blocks for success. It also helps to define weaknesses."

The major assignment in his course is to create a consumer product or service, and to market it. He encourages students to consider and try many different products, designs, or marketing strategies before settling on the final project. They also have to write two résumés: one with a list of five successes in their lives; one a list of five failures. He then asks them to think about the connections between the risks they had taken and the failures or successes in the experience. Then they give an oral presentation about their personal triumphs and setbacks. By naming these publicly, the students can again see their failures as healthy, normal, and important. One student noted that his perceived biggest failure—being laid off from his job at an oil field three years before—led to his greatest success, which was going back to school to earn an engineering degree.

Do you get discouraged when you fail? Do you ever look at your failures for the good that may have emerged from them? Even an F on a test can be a turning point to better study habits. If you have ever watched a toddler learn to walk, or a five-year-old try to ride a bike, you have seen their spirit of abandonment. Unfazed by falling, they pick themselves up, wasting little time on their failures. But something happens on the road to adulthood that causes many to freeze because of their fear of failure. It is this resistance to understanding the value of failure that Professor Matson is trying to change.

It is not just in business or engineering classes where the role of failure is a valuable learning tool. What we often think of as failure stems from simple inexperience. In any writing or public-speaking class, progress only comes about through practice and a willingness to experiment and revise. Students who resist criticism rarely advance.

Before we become too self-critical about our failures, consider that God might see these as part of something that can be turned for good. It's actually a biblical promise in Romans 8:28: "We know that in all things God works for the good of those who love him, who have been called according to his purpose." ◘

Getting Help
in Naming
the Ghosts ◘

I thought only sick or crazy people saw counselors.

A FRESHMAN

Let the wise listen and add to their learning, and let the discerning get guidance.

PROVERBS 1:5

For some students, moving away from home causes some of the troubling events of their childhoods to resurface in strange ways. It happened to Sandra when persistent nightmares began to recur for the first time in years. One particular repeating nightmare would wake her, leaving her perspiring, crying, frightened, and unable to sleep.

In her journal, she wrote:

> In my dream I see my mom driving home on the freeway, listening to her oldies station playing a Ricky Nelson tune. Then I see a large eighteen wheeler facing her from the other direction, suddenly swerving onto my mom's side of the road. It's coming straight at her tiny Toyota. Then the picture jumps to the funeral. I'm crying hard and looking at everyone. I see my dad and think about what it will be like living at his house, not with my mom. I cry even harder. In my mind I see each room of my mom's house—empty. I hear my puppy walking around, her tiny paws padding, searching for mom. Then I wake up, and it takes me a moment to assure myself it is not real. Always, I have tears.

These nightmares bothered Sandra so much that she sought help from one of the free counselors at the health center. Together they explored the details of her dreams. The counselor said that Sandra needed to "name the ghosts that were haunting her." Sandra began expressing the silent grief she had held inside since she was thirteen, when her mom and dad were divorced. Sandra told me, "My dad and I didn't have a good relationship then, but I still felt abandoned when he left. Then, I got very scared my mom would die and I worried about what would happen if I had to live with him. If she didn't come home on time, I'd panic, thinking she was in the hospital or hurt somewhere. I remembered that at thirteen, I also had dreams that Mom was in a car accident."

The counselor did not insist there was only one way to interpret the dreams, but she suggested that Sandra might try working out the fears she had never dealt with at thirteen. Said Sandra, "Our times together gave me a whole new freedom; I suddenly felt that doors were opening and I began to understand my dreams and myself. Because I asked for help, I learned so much more about myself and how I think and feel and act. I almost didn't go because I thought counselors were only for sick or crazy people."

For most students, being away from home helps them see Mom and Dad more as real people; it helps them appreciate the love that surrounds them in the family. But for some, unresolved wounds—either from divorce, family violence, neglect, incest, alcohol or drug abuse—emerge with greater intensity at a distance. Often, finding a neutral person to talk with makes a significant difference in dealing with the painful memories so they don't dominate the future. Most colleges offer free counseling, and many churches have pastors trained in listening.

But getting over stereotypes of "who sees a counselor" is often the first step. The term "Wonderful Counselor" is used in the Bible to describe Christ, and the Bible abounds with images of one person seeking wisdom and counsel from another. We are invited and encouraged to seek help at important moments in our lives.◙

Patience
with Myself ▣

*Let us run with perseverance the race that is set before us,
looking to Jesus, the pioneer and perfecter of our faith.*
HEBREWS 12:1–2 (REVISED STANDARD VERSION)

When Brian struggles with the demands of college,
he picks up his electric bass guitar and plays for a while. "It
reminds me of the advice my Dad gave me the Christmas I was
nine. He surprised me with my first electric guitar—it was so
large I could hardly get my fingers on the frets."

But the lasting gift his dad gave Brian were his words of
encouragement. "Brian, enjoy it," said his dad, who played in a
rock band during off-work hours. "Stay with it, and it will reward
you some day." So Brian did, and in a relaxed, patient way, he
practiced for years until now he is an accomplished jazz
performer, finding a lot of satisfaction in the college jazz band and
in his own musical group.

In a society that promotes instant satisfaction—the land of fast
food, fast intimacy, fast success—you may struggle with the truth
that college is often a land of slow feedback and slow progress.
Although there may be rare moments with leaps of learning, to
genuinely excel usually takes time, steady discipline, and a patient
spirit—especially toward yourself. Whether it's unraveling the
mysteries of molecular biology, crafting a powerful and precise
essay, or mastering a graceful ballet step, nothing comes easily. But
rewards do come.

For Tani, the test of patience came after graduating with a
teaching degree. "I couldn't get a job in high-school English; the
field was glutted." But she still wanted to teach, so she found a

night job on a telephone courtesy team. This freed her to take substitute teaching jobs during the day.

She loved the days she taught, and the experience reinforced her determination to keep applying for whatever openings she found. High-school English departments in her city started to request her whever they needed a substitute because students enjoyed her so much. Four years went by. Still she couldn't find a permanent position, and she kept working at night.

Finally, there was an opening in the high school where she had substituted most. As one of the two final candidates for the position, she felt she had a good chance because the staff already knew her and recommended her. Two days after the interview Tani was told, "You didn't get the job." An inside friend told her the school had hired an inexperienced teacher who happened to have skills in coaching tennis. "It was absolutely my lowest point in faith," Tani told me later. "Maybe I simply wasn't facing realities in the job market.

Shortly after that, she received a temporary six-month position, which involved moving three hundred miles away to another city. "A detour," she said, but she took it because of the school's excellent reputation. Her temporary position became full time, and her Advanced Placement students selected her as the Outstanding English Teacher of the Year. She is now listed in *Who's Who of American Teachers.* Her detour also included another surprise. If she had been given the earlier job, she would never have met the man she married last spring.

Are you ever impatient with your progress? Is there one area of your life where it could be helpful to be more gentle with yourself? ◘

Rebuilding After Failure, or the Rubble Brigade ◼

You are forgiving and good, O Lord, abounding in love to all who call to you.   PSALM 86:5

When we heard what our government did to the six million Jews in the camps, we were so ashamed.
                                        A WOMAN FROM BERLIN

When survivors emerged from the air-raid shelters and basements of Berlin on May 2, 1945, they found a vast wasteland of ruins. Over 50,000 buildings had been destroyed by allied bombings, leaving Berlin with no electricity, no gas, little running water and 75 million cubic meters of debris. The center of the city was covered with dead bodies, rubble, burned-out tanks and heavy artillery, and 3 million devastated people.

"But even more devastating than all the destruction was the shame we felt as we heard the full horror of the Nazi concentration camps," recalls one woman survivor. "A sense of national guilt overwhelmed us."

But within days, the women, hungry and exhausted, began clearing the streets. Called the "rubble brigade," they started mending and repairing, clearing away the ruins, and salvaging reusable material. Day by day, brick by brick, they worked to restore their city and their lives.

One enormous pile of rubble eventually turned into a hillside ski-run, now a popular place for college students and the host for a world-class ski competition one winter. The women turned their sorrow and shame into hope, forging something new for the war-torn city.

During this same war, a young German pastor, Dietrich Bonhoeffer, joined an underground resistance group against Hitler. Bonhoeffer was captured and imprisoned in Berlin, and executed just days before the war ended. But during those years of imprisonment, he wrote constantly to friends and family. Later these letters were gathered into the book *Letters and Papers from Prison,* which has been read around the world.

In writing about the sovereignty of God in history in 1943, he stated:

> I believe that God can and will bring good out of evil,
> even out of the greatest evil. . . . For that purpose he needs
> men who make the best use of everything. . . . I believe
> that even our mistakes and shortcomings are turned to good
> account, and that it is no harder for God to deal with
> them than our supposedly good deeds. I believe that God is
> no timeless fate, but that he waits for and answers sincere
> prayer and responsible actions.

Though the Nazis thought they had silenced him, Christians around the world still find themselves challenged by his call to commitment, expressed in his earlier book *The Cost of Discipleship* and in his letters. But even more by the way he lived out his faith.

Are there destructive actions that give shame and guilt to your days or nights, creating rubble in your own and others' lives, hindering your walk with God? Do you wonder if your own mistakes and shortcomings are too big for God's greater goodness? Why not trust the promise of forgiveness and step out with enough faith to begin picking up the pieces, one by one, so God can recreate your life? ◙

Sleep—An
Endangered Species ◘

If I sleep, I miss a lot of what's going on here.
AN EXHAUSTED FROSH, LIVING IN A LARGE DORM

One of the first temptations of college life, especially
if you live on campus, is to skimp on sleep. One student described
the effects of such a mistake this way: "My biggest source of stress
at college has been lack of sleep. This affects everything I do.
When I'm tired I procrastinate because 'I don't feel like doing it
now' (I'm too lazy). My tiredness affects my relationship with my
roommate, friends, and especially my professors, because it affects
my performance in their classes. When I'm tired my attitude tends
to be more negative than if I wasn't. I'm more impatient and short
tempered. This is something I have really started to work on, but
it's hard to go to bed because there is just so much to do! I need to
change my habits."

One professor and his wife, who often invite students to their
home, find students talk freely about the stress in their lives. When
they do, he asks, "How much sleep have you had in the last forty-
eight hours?" If they haven't been sleeping much, he says, "Get a
good night's sleep, and then let's talk about this tomorrow." In his
long experience, he inevitably finds that problems loom much
larger in students' minds, and solutions much scarcer, when they
are living on the thin edge of exhaustion.

Sometimes it's not just homework, but worry, or even
ambition, that keeps people awake. Students returning to college
at midlife often find a level of intellectual excitement and sense of
purpose that drives them with new ambition. After taking care of
children, studying, working, and attending classes, the only time to
think is at bedtime—and the mind whirls. Dom Helder Camara,

the archbishop of Recife, Brazil, writes of this in his book of poems
A Thousand Reasons for Living:

> *At least at night*
> *let your heart*
> *have a rest. . . .*
> *At least at night*
> *stop your career,*
> *calm those desires*
> *that nearly madden you,*
> *see if you can manage*
> *to put your dreams to sleep.*
> *Yield yourself*
> *body and soul,*
> *yield yourself*
> *really,*
> *truly and completely*
> *into God's hands!*

Sleep—one of the daily mundane decisions that helps preserve strength. The psalmist assures us, "He gives to his beloved sleep" (Psalm 127:2, Revised Standard Version).◙

Carving Out
Priorities ▣

The thing is to understand myself, to see what God really wishes me to do; the thing is to find a truth which is true for me.   DANISH PHILOSOPHER SØREN KIERKEGAARD

Just as students pause to clean their rooms or wash their laundry on a free Saturday afternoon, many find it helpful to take time to rethink their priorities now and then.

One Thursday night at 10:45, Lisa finally returned to her room to begin several hours of study. "I'd been to two student group meetings—one for a dorm activity, the other for a social issue—which were actually the last of several other meetings I'd attended that week," she remembers. "I came into the room really stressed, because exams and papers were coming on Friday. That night, my roommate did a wonderful thing. She simply raised a question about my choices: 'Is that really you, Lisa?' Somehow, the genuineness of her concern about my rushing around stopped me cold."

Lisa, like many other first-year students, found her new life lonely, so she filled her days with the immediate camaraderie of causes and friends. But the truth was she didn't have much interest in most of the activities she participated in. And this was leading her dangerously close to academic suicide and failing health. It caused her to skip a lot of meals and lose a lot of sleep. By mid-semester, she described herself as "an emotional wreck."

Now and then we need to take time to weed out what's important and what's not, for the clutter of too many activities can sap our energy. At times, it's hard to do this because so much is appealing and worthwhile.

Once, while attending a *Guidepost* magazine writers' workshop in New York, I heard author Elizabeth Sherril say,

> When a sculptor like Michaelangelo carves a David, or the Pietá in a beautiful piece of stone, to get at the essence of the picture, he constantly carves away good stone, letting it drop to the floor. In writing, we often have to do the same thing with fine sentences or paragraphs ... if they draw strength away from the heart of the story. It's always hard at first to let go of something good. But if we don't, we weaken the essence.

The same applies to our choices. Does this mean students shouldn't get involved in extra-curricular activities? Of course not. Outside activities are important. In fact, some people estimate that seventy percent of what students learn actually comes to them outside the classroom—through sports, activities, dorm life, and friendships.

But for Lisa, her roommate's comment caused her to reconsider: "What really matters?" Once she carved the good but unimportant activities out of her schedule, she was able to pursue her prime love—ballet. With more free time, she could prepare for the spring performance. "It allowed me to build friendships in one community, develop physical health and grace, and relieve tension. Best of all, practice times were predictable, though demanding." Her second semester proved far more satisfying, academically and personally. And a more real Lisa emerged.

Do you ever find yourself outrageously overloaded? Not just the predictable tensions during mid-term and finals weeks—but almost daily? Are you working too many hours off campus to buy things you don't really need? Or if you're a nontraditional student with family and work demands, are you academically overloaded? Sometimes changing a personal timetable and taking an extra year to earn the degree allows a lighter load each term. It can make all the difference.

Is there anything good you need to carve out? ▣

Conclusion ▫

Over the past few weeks, our old cottage home on a hillside has been in the process of being remodeled. Each day skilled carpenters enter, tear out walls, knock down ceilings, lift off leaky roofs, widen windows, pull down doors—all dirty, noisy, destructive essentials before they can rebuild. For days, an entire outside wall disappeared, with just sheets of plastic to protect the inside from wind and rain. It's messy and slow—very slow—work, especially since they've decided to take a week off to go elk hunting!

And through it all, we have needed to trust the builders' knowledge of construction, especially in determining which are the "bearing walls." Those are the walls that must remain in place because they hold up the whole structure. It is also essential to know where bearing beams must be added to withstand new construction.

Right now I hate it. I'm tired of living in chaos and clutter. At times, I long for the peace that existed before we chose to make changes, and I feel a bit like the Berliners this summer who, disturbed by the disruption, uncertainty, and rapid change in their society, started wearing T-shirts that read, "I want my wall back!"

But I don't, really. Already, we see glimpses of the new design emerging. The covered entryway is far more welcoming to guests, who used to have to climb crumbling stairs and wait unprotected from ice and snow. The higher ceilings, French doors, and bay windows that open to decks create an expansive connection to the outdoors. Now we see the majestic maples, pine, and spruces that line our country road, bringing this beauty indoors.

At times you may feel this way about the college experience. When experiences challenge our mental, emotional, and spiritual structures of life and the old interior walls start to crumble, the dismantling isn't always comfortable. And often it's slow work to build a more expansive inner and outer life, one that welcomes the world. The sense of loss, the days or months of confusion, and the need to trust in a wise Designer—and an unknown future—all this can be daunting. In building new bearing walls, you will at times long for the security of the earlier, known walls. Probably not for long, though. More often, students say they are excited by the new vistas that open.

It is a rare senior who isn't grateful for the inner changes he or she has seen during the previous four years. "It seems like I used to see in black and white and now the world's in technicolor," said one graduate.

At the end of this book, I have included a list of books by and about some of the "rare beasts" you have met in this book. I hope that you will find them important friends along the way. They could help you build new bearing walls to hold the expansion of your mind and heart. Many other excellent writers were not included, but if you look for them you will find many other people who have explored the depths of living out the Christian faith in our complex culture.

A last thought: I would welcome it if you were to write and tell me of your faith experiences. Very little has been written by college students on what their day-by-day spiritual quest involves. What encourages your faith? What doubts trouble you? What encounters with other Christians, books, music, or worship have been meaningful—or confusing—to you? What areas would you like to have heard more about from other students and "rare beasts"? Perhaps when I revise this book in the future, these ideas could be included. My address is:

Linda Lawrence
English Department
Whitworth College
Spokane, Washington 99251

Thanks. I'd love to hear from you.◙

BOOKS FOR
THE JOURNEY

ST. AUGUSTINE

The Confessions

FREDERICK BEUCHNER

Now and Then
The Sacred Journey
Telling the Truth
Wishful Thinking
Spiritual Quests: The Art and Craft of Religious Writing edited by
    William Zinsser (includes five other writers)
The Wizard's Tide
Telling Secrets

DIETRICH BONHOEFFER

Letters and Papers from Prison
Life Together
The Cost of Discipleship

DOM HELDER CAMERA

A Thousand Reasons for Living (poetry)
Helder Camera: Talks and Writings
The Impossible Dream: The Spirituality of Dom Helder Camera by
    Mary Hall
Dom Helder Camera: The Violence of a Peacemaker by José de
    Brouker

Witnesses Before Dawn: Exploring the Meaning of Christian Life by
William D. Apel (includes short biographies of Mark Hatfield,
Dietrich Bonhoeffer, and others)

DAG HAMMARSKJÖLD

Markings

SENATOR MARK HATFIELD

Between a Rock and a Hard Place
Conflict and Conscience

HILDEGARD OF BINGEN

Illuminations of Hildegard of Bingen
Hildegard of Bingen's Scivias "Know the Ways"

JULIAN OF NORWICH

Julian of Norwich: Showings, from the Classics of Western
Spirituality Series
Julian of Norwich by Brendan Doyle
Catholic Spiritual Classics by Mitch Finley (includes eleven other
writers, including: Augustine, Thomas Merton, St. Francis,
and others)

DR. MARTIN LUTHER KING, JR.

Strength to Love
Letter from a Birmingham Jail
The Trumpet Shall Sound by Stephen Oates

MADELEINE L'ENGLE

Walking on Water: Reflections on Faith and Art
A Circle of Quiet
The Irrational Season

The Summer of the Great-grandmother
And It Was Good

C. S. LEWIS

The Chronicles of Narnia
Surprised by Joy
Clive Staples Lewis: A Dramatic Life by William Griffin

CATHERINE MARSHALL

A Man Called Peter
Beyond Ourselves
The Helper

HENRI J. M. NOUWEN

The Wounded Healer
Lifesigns
Reaching Out
In the Name of Jesus: Reflections on Christian Leadership
Beyond the Mirror: Reflections on Death and Life

MOTHER TERESA

A Mother Teresa Treasury
Life in the Spirit: Reflections, Meditations, Prayers
My Life for the Poor
I Need Souls Like You
The Love of Christ: Spiritual Counsels
Something Beautiful for God by Malcolm Muggeridge

BISHOP DESMOND TUTU

Hope and Suffering: Sermons and Speeches
Tutu: Voice of the Voiceless by Shirley Du Boulay

SIMONE WEIL

Waiting for God
Simone Weil: A Life by Simone Petrement

There are so many thoughtful Christian voices left out of this short book that I think you would enjoy, it's tempting to want to keep adding to the list. Writers like Dorothy Day, Thomas Merton, Theresa of Avila, Meister Eckhart, St. John of the Cross, Matthew Fox, Elizabeth O'Conner, Tom Sine, Robert Coles, Pascal, Brother Lawrence, Robert McAfee Brown—see the danger if I get started? But it really isn't necessary; if you like reading, you'll soon discover your own favorites.

INDEX OF TOPICS DISCUSSED

forgiveness, 45, 59, 61, 66, 106, 135, 166
friendship, 23–25

giving, 144–45
goal setting, 53
guidance, 34, 53, 61, 95, 97

Hammarskjöld, Dag, 32, 51, 103, 194
Handel, George Frideric, 37
Hatfield, Mark, 26–28, 194
Hildegard of Bingen, 32–33, 194
homesickness, 22, 35, 115, 120
honesty, 62

identity, 128
images of God, 88
imagination, 89, 107, 109, 151, 166
inadequacies, 59, 68, 122–23, 164
intellectual freedom, 84
international students, 138, 147

jealousy, 128
journal keeping, 103–5
joy, 159
Julian of Norwich, 64–65, 194

kayaking, 113–14
kindness, 159
King, Dr. Martin Luther, Jr., 67–70, 77, 194

L'Engle, Madeleine, 83, 95, 194
Lewis, C. S., 71–73, 78, 195
leadership, 29–30
love, biblical description, 139

Marshall, Catherine, 40–43, 195
moodiness, 37, 128, 171
money, 37, 40–42, 63, 136, 144, 178
Mother Teresa, 158–60, 195
motherhood of God, 64

nuclear disarmament, 27, 107–9

obedience, 73

patience, 81, 117, 151, 183
physical fitness, 113, 127–28
politics and faith, 26–27, 77, 103
prayer, 40, 60, 68, 100, 123, 159
pride and humility, 36, 53, 73, 110, 117, 123, 148
priorities, 30, 189–90

rejection, 24, 28
religious prejudice, 147
restlessness, 59
rock climbing, 90

science, 82–83
self-acceptance, 29, 164–65
self-centeredness, 72, 104–5, 138

INDEX OF TOPICS DISCUSSED